THE CONVERGENT CHURCH

Moving Toward the Unity for Which Jesus Prayed

Peter DeHaan

ISBN:
979-8-88809-073-2 (paperback)
979-8-88809-074-9 (hardcover

Published by Rock Rooster Books, Grand Rapids, Michigan

ABSTRACT

THE CONVERGENT CHURCH: MOVING TOWARDS THE UNITY FOR WHICH JESUS PRAYED

Peter Lyle DeHaan, PhD
Trinity College of the Bible and Trinity Theological Seminary
Chair: Dr. Katheryn L. Webb

Keywords: church unity, Christian unity, ecumenical, postmodern, emerging church, emergent church, Great Emergence, Holy Spirit, Trinity, Trinitarianism, convergent church, Great Convergence

In John 17, Jesus prayed for unity among all who would follow Him. The purpose for this concord of His supporters was so that the world would know Him and the Father. Jesus realized that harmony among His future followers would be essential in order to maximize the effectiveness of their witness to the world. Conversely, if His adherents were divided, disagreeing with one another, the efficacy of their testimony would be tarnished and greatly diminished.

The fact that this prayer was Jesus' final act as a free man demonstrates the critical importance He placed on the concurrence of His disciples, both present and future. While this unity was largely realized by the early church, the subsequent two millennia have been increasingly characterized by persistent disunity and polarized division. This is prominently evidenced by the major divisions within Christianity and epitomized by 42,000 disagreeing Protestant denominations.

Modernity and the age of enlightenment advanced the intellectual conviction that, through careful analytical study and discourse, an ultimate and singular knowledge could be ascertained. This principle held hope for a theological melding of church theology to transpire. However, the opposite occurred, with divergent and polarizing pronouncements made with increased regularity over the past 500 years. Modernity spawned significant spiritual division, and the church took a beating under its rule.

Paradoxically, it is postmodernity – with its twin attributes of tolerance and inclusiveness – that holds the potential for the reunification of Jesus' followers. This is exemplified by the perspectives and practices of the emerging church and the emergent church, as well as house churches and various parachurch movements. Phyllis Tickle advocates that the Christian church is on the cusp of a "Great Emergence"[1] that could surpass the Great Reformation in terms of both scope and influence.

A recurring theme in these recent developments is the present and persistent reality and work of the Holy Spirit. As such, there is a need for modern-thinking Christians to reclaim Him, rescuing Him from the clutches of modernity, which had successfully sidelined Him as it elevated the observable and quantifiable, while stifling all that was spiritual. This trend and need to re-elevate the position of the Holy Spirit can be ably bolstered by all Christians, regardless of heritage or practice, through adopting a balanced and truly Trinitarian pursuit of God.

With the inevitability of postmodernity, the envisioned Great Emergence of the Christian church, and an intentional quest for a truly holistic pursuit of God as Trinity, a convergence is taking place. This is a convergence of Jesus' followers, working together regardless of their respective historical traditions and preferential theologies for the common goal of effectively reaching the world for Him. As a result, the church of Jesus can become the unified witness that He desired and prayed for in earnest. This is the convergent church, the Great

---

1. Phyllis Tickle, The Great Emergence (Grand Rapids, MI: Baker Books, 2008), 13-17, 162-163.

Convergence.

THE CONVERGENT CHURCH: MOVING TOWARDS THE UNITY FOR WHICH JESUS PRAYED

DISSERTATION

Submitted to the Faculty
in partial fulfillment of the requirements
for the degree of

DOCTOR OF PHILOSOPHY IN PASTORAL MINISTRY
at Trinity College of the Bible and Trinity Theological Seminary

By

Peter Lyle DeHaan

Newburgh, Indiana
April 2012

THE CONVERGENT CHURCH

CONTENTS

CHAPTER 1: INTRODUCTION

The Research Problem

The Research Problem

The last thing Jesus did as a free man, before He was arrested and executed, was pray. In His prayer, which is recorded in John 17, He first prayed for Himself, then for His disciples, and lastly for all who would believe in Him. "These words," says Ken Sande in his book *The Peacemaker*, "apply directly to every Christian today.[1] In this, Jesus petitioned that His followers would be one, just as He and the Father are one.[2] More directly, Jesus asked that His followers be "brought to complete unity" (John 17:23).[3] Succinctly stated, *"Jesus prayed that his followers would get*

---

1. Ken Sande, The Peacemaker, 4th ed. (Grand Rapids, MI: Baker Books, 2005), 47.

2. Frank Viola and George Barna, Pagan Christianity? (USA: Tyndale House Publishers Inc, 2008), 191.

3. John F. Walvoord, and Roy B. Zuck. The Bible Knowledge Commentary. (Colorado Springs, CO: David C. Cook, 1983), 333-334; John McArthur. The McArthur Bible Commentary. (Nashville, TN: Thomas Nelson, 2005), 1412.

along with one another."[4] Notably, this was Jesus' longest recorded prayer[5] and His most passionate one.[6]

Jesus' appeal for unity was not merely so that harmony and peace would be realized, but rather for the higher purpose of reaching the world for Him (John 17:23).[7] He affirmed that the effectiveness of spreading the gospel was ultimately contingent on the unity of His followers. Therefore, the ultimate purpose of unity was to facilitate the best possible Christian witness. If, then, there is to be greater success in fulfilling the great commission of making disciples of the entire world (Matthew 28:19-20),[8] which appears to be their primary purpose for being, the effort would be best served by unity among all believers.[9]

Disunity among Christians serves as a constraint in reaching the world for Jesus. The prevailing question then becomes, will the church come together in unity irrespective of theological disagreements or will it allow doctrinal differences to cause division, disregarding Jesus' prayer and wish for His followers?[10] Simply stated, "We should be careful not to separate ourselves from our brothers and our sisters."[11]

---

4. Sande 2005, 48.

5. Tony Dale, Felicity Dale, and George Barna, The Rabbit and the Elephant (USA: Barna Books / Tyndale House Publishers, 2009), 167.

6. Dale 2009, 195.

7. Walvoord 1983, 334; McArthur 2005, 1414.

8. Dale 2009, 86; Dan Kimball, The Emerging Church (Grand Rapids, MI: Zondervan, 2003), 64-65, 214.

9. Kimball 2003, 93.

10. Dale 2009, 167.

11. Ibid., 195.

Jesus Prays for Unity

John recorded that as Jesus prepared to celebrate the Passover – His final Passover on earth and just prior to His crucifixion – "Jesus knew that the time had come for Him to leave this world and go to the Father" (John 13:1). Jesus could have prioritized His final moments in any manner: to say good-bye to His family and friends, to give final instructions to His disciples, or even to rest in anticipation of the ordeal ahead. Instead, He opted to pray, withdrawing to Gethsemane for a time of intense communication with His Father in heaven (Matthew 26:36, Mark 14:32).

In this prayer, which the eyewitness John recorded, Jesus first prayed for Himself (John 17:1-5),[12] then for His disciples (John 17:6-17),[13] and lastly for all who would believe in Him (John 17:20-26).[14] As His last petition, it was perhaps the most important, being emphasized and elevated over the others;[15] the words apply directly to His church today.[16] Jesus prayed to His Father for His future followers. He asked that they would be one, just as He and the Father are one, which is to say that they will be unified (John 17:20-21).[17] Jesus was calling them "to live by divine life," notes Frank Viola, "the same life that exists within the

---

12. McArthur 2005, 1412.

13. Brian D. McLaren, Everything Must Change (Nashville, TN: Thomas Nelson, 2007), 114.

14. Walvoord 1983, 333.

15. Phillip Yancey, "Denominational Diagnostics," Christianity Today (November 2008): 119.

16. Sande 2005, 47.

17. Walvoord 1983, 333.

Godhead."[18]

Jesus said, "I pray also for those who will believe in me through their message" (John 17:20), that they will be "brought to complete unity to let the world know that you sent me and have loved them" (John 17:23).[19] The word *know* is alternately rendered as *believe* (John 17:23, MSG). The unity among Jesus' followers, then, is for the express purpose that the world may know and believe.

The Purpose of Unity

The unity Jesus desired was not merely for the sake of getting along, enjoying a harmonious existence, or experiencing interpersonal peace, but rather for a higher purpose of effectuating an optimal witness of Him to others. When seeking the unity for which Jesus prayed, the perspective today should be the same. It is not merely desiring unity for unity's sake, but enhancing the efficacy of reaching a world that does not follow Jesus.[20]

Jesus equated the unity of His followers to His oneness with His Father, petitioning that "all of them may be one, Father, just as you are in me and I am in you" (John 17:21).[21] Indeed, just as the Father and the Son are one, so should those who follow the Son be one. In like manner as there is unity within the Godhead, there ought to be unity among the followers of Jesus; that is, His church.[22]

The unity that Jesus sought for His disciples when He said, "Holy Father, protect them by the power of your name ... so that they may be one as we

---

18. Frank Viola, Reimagining Church (Colorado Springs: David C. Cook, 2008), 226.

19. McArthur 2005, 1414.

20. Sande 2005, 47.

21. McArthur 2005, 1414.

22. Viola 2008, 92.

are one" (John 17:11)[23] found evidence of fulfillment in the book of Acts and throughout the New Testament Epistles.[24] Although the early church struggled with conflicts, disagreements, and differences, these were confronted and corrected. The drive for and realization of unity is an overarching and pervasive trait throughout the New Testament.

The Future Focus of Unity

The future-focused portion of this unity – for "those who will believe" (John 17:20) – still awaits full realization, as disunity in the church increased during the ensuing 2,000 years. Steadily over time the followers of Jesus have given in to increased fragmentation and polarization, vilifying, hating, and even killing each other. Tactfully sparing the details, Phyllis Tickle, who calls herself a professional religionist,[25] concisely indicates that this disunity has "a bloody history."[26] Major disparate derivations of belief grew within Christianity, especially within the Protestant branch with its 42,000 doctrinally sparring and culturally segregated

---

23. Ibid.

24. The supporting verses are numerous and will be detailed in Chapter 2, "Biblical Support for Unity."

25. Phyllis Tickle, The Words of Jesus (San Francisco: Jossey-Bass, 2008), 3.

26. Phyllis Tickle, The Great Emergence (Grand Rapids, MI: Baker Books, 2008), 46.

denominations.[27] This present-day reality[28] is far from the unity the Jesus desired for His followers and for which He passionately prayed (John 17).

The Importance of Unity

Itinerate revivalist John Crowder puts the importance of church unity poignantly into perspective. "If we are not walking in unity with the body," he warns, "then we are not walking in full unity with Christ."[29] The fundamental purpose of unity is to bear fruit in other areas; unity requires that people actually "do things together," not just gather for a citywide joint meeting – although that is a good starting initiative.[30] Crowder notes that unity is respectful of where each follower of Jesus is in his or her own personal spiritual journey; unity trusts God's leading in their lives and is not judgmental. Unity also accepts and embraces the individual gifts and specific ministries of others who are different, without requiring conformity in either style or function.[31]

To realize this imperative for unity, a requisite value needs to be granted to each Christian, seeing "the eternal worth of Christ that has been placed upon

---

27. Ted Olsen, "Go Figure,"
    http://www.christianitytoday.com/ct/2011/april/gofigure-apr11.html,
    (accessed April 2, 2012) and "Status of Global Mission, 2011, in Context of
    20th and 21st Centuries,"
    http://www.gordonconwell.edu/resources/documents/StatusOfGlobalMi
    ssion.pdf, (accessed April 2, 2012).

28. Viola and Barna 2008, 249-250; Dale 2009, 154; Wolfgang Simson, The
    House Church Book (USA: Tyndale/Barna Books, 2009), xx-xxi.

29. John Crowder, Miracle Workers, Reformers, and the New Mystics
    (Shippensburg, PA: Destiny Publishers Inc, 2006), 270.

30. Ibid., 272.

31. Ibid., 270.

him."[32] Unity, therefore, requires a change in perspective, one that can only find fulfillment in a mutual, genuine love for others. "Unity itself is not really the ultimate goal; love is the goal," Crowder states. "Unity is just the fruit of love. We may completely despise one another's calling, function, and ministry tactics, but if we have love for each another anyway, we can still achieve unity."[33] Parallel to the aforementioned statement of purpose, so that "the world may believe" (John 17:23, MSG), Crowder advocates a progression: intimacy with God leads to purity; purity produces unity; from unity springs revival.[34]

Historical Movements Toward Disunity

Much has happened between Jesus' pointed prayer for the unity of His followers and the reality in which His church finds itself today. The church has moved away from unity and moved toward disunity, specializing in schisms while increasing religious polarization and quarrels among those who follow Jesus. American religion scholar Diana Butler Bass notes that, throughout Christian history, "the church has never gotten it completely right." She does add, however, that the church "has not gotten it completely wrong either."[35]

Five Hundred Year Shifts

In her book *The Great Emergence: How Christianity Is Changing and Why*, Phyllis Tickle asserts that seismic shifts in religious thought and practice

---

32. Ibid.

33. Ibid.

34. Ibid., 269.

35. Diana Butler Bass, A People's History of Christianity (New York: HarperOne, 2009), 17.

recur with measurable regularity.[36] Disunity increases with each transition. "The church," Tickle states, "undergoes a change about every 500 years."[37] She characterizes these periodic "re-formations" as having a confluence of contributing factors that produce a chaotic revolution of events.[38] Tickle notes that at each transition, the then current form of organized Christian faith is not destroyed by one of these "semi-millennial eruptions." Rather, it continues on, albeit with lessening influence and diminished pride, as it is compelled to yield to the new form of faith as it is being birthed. These old forms do not cease to exist, but do persist into the future, carrying with them their traditions of the past, while simultaneously developing new ones for the future.[39]

Tickle's 500-year intervals, spanning two millennia of Christianity, are marked by the Birth of Christianity (Jesus),[40] Gregory the Great (the Council of Chalcedon, circa 590),[41] the Great Schism (the east-west split of Christianity in 1054),[42] the Great Reformation (Martin Luther in 1517),[43] and the Great Emergence (the present time).[44] These changes are not limited to the two millennia of Christianity. Tickle notes that Jews would see the Babylonian

---

36. Tickle 2008, Emergence, 16.

37. Phyllis Tickle, "Ancient Disciplines for the Church" (audio sermon podcast, Mars Hill Bible Church, June 29, 2008).

38. Tickle 2008, Emergence, 22.

39. Ibid., 27.

40. Ibid., 26.

41. Ibid., 22-23.

42. Ibid., 20.

43. Ibid., 19-20, 43-44.

44. Ibid., 41-42, 120.

Captivity preceding Jesus by 500 years and the age of the Judges ending 500 years before that; it is a Judeo-Christian pattern.[45] Furthermore, she asserts that a good Muslim would see the same 500-year pattern, an Abrahamic pattern.[46]

Humanity, she notes, has a need to institutionalize, which snowballs for about 500 years until an upheaval occurs. At each transition, Tickle indicates that the dominant form of thought loses hegemony. It does not cease to be; it merely loses its dominance. The former way continues to exist, albeit with lesser influence, but it may also change, just as the Roman Catholic Church did after the Reformation.[47]

It is important to realize that these shifts do not occur abruptly on a specific date, but build up over time, erupt, and then move forward.[48] As exemplified by the Reformation, three outcomes result from each shift: (1) a more vital form of Christianity emerges, (2) the once-dominant form reconstitutes itself into a purer version of its former existence, and (3) faith spreads.[49] According to Tickle, the world is once again in the midst of one of these landmark events; it is "a time of enormous change."[50] Diana Butler Bass calls this phenomenon a "retraditioning,"[51] which Tickle echoes.[52] Bass states that retraditioning is a "simpler concept" than what the name might imply. She indicates that it is a

---

45. Ibid., 29.

46. Ibid., 30.

47. Ibid., 28.

48. Tickle 2008, Ancient; Tickle 2008, Emergence, 17.

49. Tickle 2008, Emergence, 16-17.

50. Tickle 2008, Ancient.

51. Diana Butler Bass, The Practicing Congregation (Herndon, VA: The Alban Institute, 2004), 47-50.

52. Tickle 2008, Emergence, 28.

"process wherein individuals – and congregations – are responding to the larger cultural results of modern fragmentation," the result of which is "pockets" of Christian practitioners reconnecting with Christianity's long history of "witness and practice in a disconnected world."[53]

Bass's own model of church history is not dissimilar to Tickle's. In parallel fashion, Bass chronicles these moves in blocks of time in her book *A People's History of Christianity: The Other Side of the Story*. She details the eras of "Early Christianity" (100 to 500), "Medieval Christianity" (500 to 1450), "Reformation Christianity" (1450 to 1650), "Modern Christianity" (1650 to 1945), and "Contemporary Christianity" (1945 to present).[54]

Don Kimble advances a nearly identical schema, using the labels "Early Church" (the first century to 500), "Middle Ages" (500 to 1500), and "Modern Era" (1500 to the present), with a current transitioning into postmodernity and stretching into the future.[55]

With dates that serve only as an approximate and imprecise guide,[56] these three timelines are essentially in agreement, having only two minor differences in grouping. Tickle splits the Medieval Era (500 to 1450) into two segments, divided by the Great Schism (1054). Conversely, Tickle and Kimble combine Bass's Reformation Christianity (1450 to 1650) with Modern Christianity (1650 to 1945) for one era that starts with the Great Reformation (1517) and ends with the Great Emergence (the present time).

Using Tickle's classification schema, an expanded explanation of each era will be presented, beginning with the movement that Jesus started. From that baseline, each subsequent 500-year shift will result in increased disunity.

---

53. Bass 2004, 50.

54. Bass 2009, History, 17-18.

55. Crowder 2006, 37-39.

56. Tickle 2008, Emergence, 17.

Jesus' Ministry and the Birth of Christianity

Judaism at the time of Jesus centered on three essential elements of faith and practice: worship at the Temple, the ministrations of priests, and the required offering of sacrifices. Jesus simultaneously replaced and personally fulfilled all three.[57] Therefore, the life of Jesus, starting with His public ministry and teachings and culminating in His death and resurrection, served as the birth of Christianity. This event was so significant that time was subsequently reordered to correspond to His birth.[58] This first era of Christianity is called the early church, the ancient church, or early Christianity, and roughly lasted for the next 500 years. The time was "messy, chaotic, violent,"[59] and in many ways foreign to the comprehension of twenty-first century humanity. Followers pursued Christianity as a present, practical way of life, not as something theoretical or future-focused. In doing so, they formed a unique social group with its own behavioral code and values. Perhaps most notable was its inclusive nature, serving to encourage diversity. It was a time when conversion was costly and included the possibility of martyrdom. Interestingly, it was at this time that the label *Christian*, meaning "little Christ," was contemptibly and disparagingly bestowed on the early followers of Jesus by their Roman detractors.[60]

Jesus' ministry and the formation of the early church, covering approximately the first 100 years of this era, are chronicled in the biblical accounts. The first century church was the church of Jesus in its purest form, before it became tainted and corrupted.[61] At that time, the greatest degree of unity existed, but it decreased progressively in the two millennia that followed.

---

57. Viola 2008, 10-11.

58. Tickle 2008, Emergence, 26.

59. Ibid.

60. Bass 2009, History, 25-35.

61. Viola and Barna 2008, xviii.

The values and practices of the early church remained intact, largely because they were a persecuted sect.[62] This persecution became increasingly vigorous, in part because of the Christians' adamant claim to possess exclusive truth in a pluralistic world. With postmodernity's rejection of absolute truth, one wonders if tomorrow's Christians will be faced with an equally intense persecution.[63]

It was during this time, notes Rick Warren, that the church was led by a group of amateurs – not trained, paid clergy. This type of church structure continued for the next 300 years.[64]

The Influence of Constantine

By the fourth century, many followers of Jesus fled to the desert to pursue a life of holiness and live in relative safety.[65] However, when Emperor Constantine converted to Christianity and made it the official religion of the Roman Empire,[66] Christians quickly became a favored majority instead of a persecuted minority.[67] Although well intentioned, Constantine's efforts to promote his newfound faith resulted in the institutionalization of Christian practices,[68] including the construction of state-sponsored cathedrals, the displacement of house churches,

---

62. Bass 2009, History, 66.

63. Daniel Egeler, Mentoring Millennials (Colorado Springs: Navpress, 2003), 65,

64. Timothy C. Morgan, "After the Aloha Shirts," Christianity Today (October 2008): 44.

65. Crowder 2006, 65; Bass 2009 History, 47.

66. Bass 2009, History, 67; Viola and Barna 2008, 18-19; Simson 2009, 19.

67. Dale 2009, 25.

68. Bass 2009, History, 63 & 67.

and the establishment of a "professional priesthood"[69] to replace the priesthood of all believers.[70] Frank Viola sees significant roots of church division – that is, disunity – emanating from the unbiblical[71] distinction between the laity and the clergy that was inadvertently instituted at this time. This division spawned "a self-perpetuating movement" that reproduced a plethora of "new sects in every generation." The new sects were more leader-driven and personality-centered than Christ-focused.[72]

Also attributable to Constantine was the halt of widespread persecution of Christians, but at the cost of injecting a political spirit into the church, which remains intact to the present day.[73] Without a doubt, "Constantine's preempting of Christianity" was monumentally pivotal, thrusting it into the role of a dominant institution. At this point, the "Hellenization of the faith" began "to accelerate, infiltrate, and eventually dominate Christian theology,"[74] with the church of Jesus absorbing both Jewish and pagan practices.[75]

Council of Chalcedon

The next era began with "Gregory the Great" (more properly, Gregory I or St. Gregory I). This period is alternately known as "The Fall of the Roman Empire" or "The Coming of the Dark Ages."

---

69. Viola and Barna 2008, 13.

70. Viola and Barna 2008, 12-13, 21, 115, 117, 247-248; the doctrine of the priesthood of all believers is found in 1 Peter 2:4-5, 9.

71. See chapter 5 in Pagan Christianity?

72. Viola 2008, 122.

73. Crowder 2006, 38.

74. Tickle 2008, Emergence, 161.

75. Viola and Barna 2008, 13.

Gregory was born around 540 and became pope fifty years hence. As pope, Gregory realized that for unity to exist within the church, allowances were needed for diversity.[76] He advocated unification in Jesus and the sacraments, while allowing for diversification in "customs, languages, and individual personalities."[77] The greatness attributed to him is not from his birthing of a revolution, but rather for his "brilliance in cleaning one up."

In the fifth century, with the Roman Empire dying or dead, the Council of Chalcedon was convened by the Eastern emperor Marcian to ascertain what constituted correct doctrine and what comprised heresy. Vociferous debate and dissension ensued at the council, rendering consensus unattainable.[78] The first major movement towards Christian disunity was about to take place.

As a result, "Oriental Christianity was exiled from (or withdrew from, depending on one's point of view) both Western Christianity and Eastern Christianity."[79] This marked the origins of what would later become the three major divisions of Christian faith: Western Christianity (now comprising Roman Catholicism and Protestantism), Eastern Orthodoxy (also known as Greek Orthodoxy), and Oriental Orthodoxy (alternately known as the Oriental Orthodox Church; Oriental Orthodoxy currently moves under the banners of Coptic, Ethiopian, Armenian, and Syrian Christianity).[80] At this point, it was Gregory who began the foundation on which "Western Christianity would be held in trust," albeit imperfectly, by the monks and nuns residing in Europe's

---

76. Chris R. Armstrong, Patron Saints for Postmoderns, (Downers Grove, IL: Intervarsity Press, 2009), 43.

77. Ibid., 55.

78. Tickle 2008, Emergence, 21-23.

79. Ibid., 24.

80. Ibid.

monasteries and convents.[81] The Dark Ages ensued, setting the stage for the next movement of disunity.

The Great Schism

Half a millennia later, the Great Schism occurred. Regarding this, Tickle writes, "In 1054, the Patriarch of Greek or Eastern Orthodox Christianity [Michael I Cerularius] had his anathemas and [Pope] Leo IX had his bulls of excommunication. The Patriarch had Constantinople and the Pope had Rome." The Constantinople coalition spoke Greek and preferred leavened bread for Mass; they believed that God the Father was the sole provider of the Holy Spirit. The Roman bloc used Latin and unleavened bread for their celebration of Mass; they asserted that the Holy Spirit proceeded equally from both God the Father and God the Son.[82]

With this discord brewing for more than a century over the *Filioque* – the assertion that the source and provision of the Holy Spirit proceeds from Jesus as well as from the Father – a power struggle resulted, with mutual excommunication of the leaders of both factions.[83] Hence, Roman Catholicism and Eastern Orthodoxy parted company; it was essentially an "East-West split."[84] The Eastern Church became "pluralistic and elder-driven." The author of an article in *Relevant* magazine writes that it "is not based on buildings, budgets or big shots. It is focused on obedience to the Gospel, not just knowledge

---

81. Ibid., 25-26.

82. Ibid., 20-21.

83. Ibid.

84. Brian D. McLaren, A Generous Orthodoxy (Grand Rapids, MI: Zondervan, 2004), 63.

of the Gospel."[85] Over time, the Eastern Orthodox family of faith grew to include Greek Orthodox, Russian Orthodox, Serbian Orthodox, and Antiochian Orthodox communities, along with others within their spiritual pedigree. They collectively venerate the Trinity – the Father, Son, and Holy Spirit – not in theological abstraction, but powerfully and dynamically.[86]

This was the second significant movement of disunity. At this point, the Western offshoot – that is, the Roman Catholic Church, which was centered in Europe – was primed for the next major movement of discord.[87] The church grew increasingly rich. Early in this era, Francis of Assisi challenged the status quo, among other things calling for a return to the practice of poverty and helping the poor.[88]

The Great Reformation

Over the next 500 years, another movement of dissension mounted, which ultimately produced the Great Reformation. This was not a singular historical event, but rather the compilation of a series of reformations in reaction to Catholic practices of that day.[89] It emanated from leaders such as John Wycliffe, Thomas Müntzer, Huldrych Zwingli, John Knox, John Calvin, and Richard Hooker, but it is Martin Luther's actions to which this historical movement is pinned. Specifically, the Great Reformation is dated from October 31, 1517, when Luther nailed his ninety-five theses to the door of the church in

---

85. Jaeson Ma, "The Reverse Flow of Missions," Relevant (January/February 2010): 57. (It is unclear whether Jaeson Ma is the author or merely the source for this article.)

86. McLaren 2004, 62.

87. Tickle 2008, Emergence, 19.

88. Bass 2009, History, 141.

89. Ibid., 161.

Wittenberg, Germany.[90] Interestingly, over time the Roman Catholic Church would grow to accept most of these protestations, ultimately acting to reform their own practices,[91] including private devotion, the corporate celebration of Mass, purgatory, and "dozens of other things."[92] Tickle insightfully calls this subsequent response of the Roman Catholic Church to the Reformation a "counter-reformation" or a "Catholic Reformation," depending on one's perspective.[93] With painful irony, McLaren notes, "The average Roman Catholic today sees indulgences the same way Protestants will someday see their schmaltzy religious broadcasting or pop-atonement theology (what Dallas Willard calls "the gospel of sin management") with embarrassment.... We Protestants have come darn near to selling indulgences ourselves (have you watched religious TV lately?)."[94]

As part of the Reformation, Protestants rejected their medieval heritage, reclaiming "the Roman emphasis on rhetoric alone."[95] Roman Catholic worship, which centered on the wonderment of the Mass, was replaced, courtesy of the reformers, by worship centered on words, which were preached and prayed in the language of the people.[96]

The date marking the beginning of Protestantism cannot be accurately ascertained, even though October 31, 1517, is the one assigned to it for the sake of convenience. Likewise, it is Luther's name that is most generally connected

---

90. Tickle 2008, Emergence, 20.

91. Bass 2009, History, 178; also McLaren 2004, 138-139.

92. Tickle 2008, Emergence, 58.

93. Ibid., 57.

94. McLaren 2004, 138-139.

95. Bass 2009, History, 104.

96. Ibid., 166.

with the Protestant reformation, but the aforementioned Wycliffe, Müntzer, Zwingli, Knox, Calvin, and Hooker also played key roles in the birth of this movement. Regardless, it was out of the protestation of the Roman Catholic Church, that Protestantism was birthed.[97] These Protestants, which included the Anabaptists ("more radical members of the Reformation"[98]), ultimately left the Roman Catholic Church when their concerns were not heard or reconciled,[99] the outcome of which was that over time Christianity became a truly global religion.[100]

With the Council of Chalcedon ("Gregory the Great") representing the first major split of Christendom and the Great Schism being the second, the birth of Protestantism marked the third major split, but more changes were to follow within the Protestant movement. After protesting against the excesses of Catholicism, the Protestants began protesting against each other,[101] and denominationalism replaced the state church.[102] This denominationalism served to produce even greater disunity within Christendom,[103] contrary to the example and practice of the early Christian church, which remained unified and did not divide itself into denominations.[104] This nascent Protestant Reformation was in part a movement of Christianity becoming "post-medieval" or "modern."[105]

---

97. Tickle 2008, Emergence, 20.

98. McLaren 2004, 224.

99. McLaren 2004, 63.

100. Tickle 2008, Emergence, 28.

101. McLaren 2004, 137.

102. C. Peter Wagner, Changing Church (Ventura, CA: Regal Books, 2004), 25.

103. Tickle 2008, Emergence, 46.

This modern era paved the way for the Age of Enlightenment (also called the "Age of Reason"[106]);[107] it was a celebration of human logic and values. Enlightenment viewed intellect and logic as superior, trumping emotion and subjective experience. Reality must be capable of tangible measurement. If something cannot be seen, heard, smelled, tasted, or touched, then it is not real.[108]

The church blindly followed the ideals of Enlightenment, reforming the faith experience into a rational, empirical, and somewhat scientifically based intellectualism;[109] thus, it reworked its theology and de-emphasized the supernatural facets of faith.[110] With a heavy emphasis placed on analytical thinking, Enlightenment relied on logic and reason, relegating the supernatural to superstition and exchanging spiritual experience for a systematic theology.[111]

With this Enlightenment perspective, it is not unexpected that Protestants hold the Bible in greater esteem than perhaps any other Christian faction. As a result, much of their biblical scholarship is motivated by the desire to justify their own theology and discredit the interpretation of others[112] – or more pointedly, to justify the theology of their own denomination or local church in contrast to

---

106. Crowder 2006, 39.

107. J. Lee Grady, The Holy Spirit Is Not for Sale (Grand Rapids, MI: Chosen Books, 2010), 13.

108. Paul Vieira, Jesus Has Left the Building (Woodland Park, CO: Karis Publishing, 2006), 77.

109. Bass 2009, History, 237-238.

110. Ibid., 215

111. Crowder 2006, 39.

112. McLaren 2004, 138.

that of other denominations or local churches.[113] More disunity ensued. It is no wonder that Professor Stanley Hauerwas opined that the Enlightenment was not good for Christianity and that "modernity was a theological mistake."[114]

Diana Butler Bass indicates that central to this modern mindset was the presumed and underlying understanding that religious truth is a singular truth that can be definitively ascertained. Given time, right-thinking believers expected to be able to experience a convergence of thought, producing an agreement of faith – at least in theory. However, the actual result was quite different, with a divergence of thought and much conflict among religious thinkers, each of whom deemed himself or herself to possess the correct and ultimate doctrine. This resulted in "a multitude of schisms and bitter theological arguments between Christians over the basic tenets of their faith. This divergence of theological thought provided the foundation for subsequent division within Protestantism, from which denominations would begin to emerge.[115]

As Christianity migrated to North America and developed over time, the denominational structure became the "standard fixture of church life in America for over 300 years."[116] In practice, these denominations were actually based more on heritage than theology, with sociologists asserting that their primary differences were not doctrinal but sociologically based.[117] Bass concurs, noting that the Protestant style of "accidental churchgoing" that was practiced during this time was not theological in nature and transcends denominations.[118]

---

113. Bass 2009, History, 241-242.

114. Ibid., 216. Bass cites part of a lecture by Hauerwas that she overheard while attempting to teach her own class.

115. Ibid., 289.

116. Wagner 2004, 46.

117. Ibid., 76.

118. Bass 2004, 79.

Two Factions of Protestantism Emerge

Two camps of Protestantism began to surface in the 1800s, bearing many labels but commonly referred to as "liberal" and "conservative."[119] The fundamentalist (that is, conservative) movement was birthed in response to perceived threats – that is, "liberalizing trends" – to the essential elements of Christian faith that resulted from the influences of modernism and the Enlightenment on the church. In 1910, the Presbyterian Church's General Assembly, which was likely the first to use the word "fundamentalist," advanced five faith fundamentals: 1) the inspiration and inerrancy of Scripture, 2) the divinity of Jesus, 3) the virgin birth, 4) Jesus' substitutionary atonement, and 5) the bodily resurrection and future return of Jesus.[120]

Tension increased between the two camps, effectively resulting in a religious "two-party" system in the United States. Conservatives (that is, evangelicals or fundamentalists) contended against liberals (that is, modernists or progressives) for "political and theological control of the Protestant denominations."[121] Regarding the use of the word "progressive" in the preceding delineation, Bass indicates that in recent years, the phrase "spiritual progressive" has gained favor over the label "religious liberal."[122]

With these two groups – conservative and liberal – the former was vilified by the latter as being "rigid, narrow-minded, moralistic fanatics."[123] The

---

119. McLaren 2004, 63.

120. Dan Kimball, They Like Jesus But Not the Church (Grand Rapids, MI: Zondervan, 2007), 188-189.

121. Bass 2004, 71.

122. Bass 2009, History, 53.

123. Bass 2004, 72.

conservative camp returned the favor by disparaging liberals as being "immoral, loose, biblically illiterate, and unsaved."[124] Albeit positively stated, the two groups' self-ascribed characteristics were equaling contrasting, with the liberal faction calling themselves "open-minded, progressive, and justice-oriented" and their evangelical counterparts opting for "Bible-believing, fundamental, and evangelizing."[125] Regardless of how the labels were presented, the divisions already existing in traditional sectarianism were further exacerbated by this left/right, liberal/conservative polarization.[126]

The two sets of characterizations contained both truth and error, with nothing substantial to be gained by further exploring their charges and countercharges. Disunity reigned. Bass cites studies showing that roughly 10 percent of Protestants align themselves with one of the two extremes, with the remaining 80 percent existing in the continuum between. This suggests a need to end the "two-party paradigm"; it is dysfunctional, if not dead. Postmodernity demands something new.[127]

The result, notes Lydia Bean, is a polarized division in Protestantism between those who advocate evangelism and those who espouse social justice.[128] Although both the evangelical camp and the liberal mainline group can cite biblical support for their respective positions, "neither side has the whole Gospel."[129] In using the biblical mandate as supporting fodder in the battle for their preferred perspectives, many, notes Doug Pagitt, overemphasize the

---

124. Ibid.

125. Grady 2010, Holy Spirit, 41.

126. Bass 2009, History, 290.

127. Bass 2004, 75-76.

128. Lydia Bean, "Bridging the Great Divide," Sojourners (March 2009): 23.

129. Ibid., 24.

"teaching about Jesus to the exclusion of the call to kingdom life."[130]

The Pentecostal and Charismatic Movement

The next major player was pentecostalism.[131] Further exacerbating this disunity, the pentecostal movement began in the early 1900s, separating itself from conservative Protestants (also called evangelicals).[132] They emphasized "the ecstatic work of the Holy Spirit."[133] Pentecostalism's start is traced to 1906 when African-American preacher William Seymour proclaimed a theology of the baptism of the Holy Spirit and speaking in tongues. The evidential manifestation of the gift of tongues was a shocking development to locals in Los Angeles, drawing folks from both the Negro and Latino communities, as well as Caucasians, making the gathering transcendent of race and social class. The movement relocated to 312 Azusa Street on April 14, 1906, and the pentecostal movement was birthed.[134] It is critical to point out that this was not about a theological reformation, says Crowder, but rather a restoration of re-introducing the church to its latent spiritual gifts.[135] It was an invitation for all who seek a "vibrant faith," through Jesus and "the power of the Holy Spirit."[136]

From this nascent event sprang pentecostalism, followed by the broader group

---

130. Doug Pagitt, Reimaging Spiritual Formation (Grand Rapids, MI: Zondervan, 2003), 31.

131. Tickle 2008, Emergence, 83.

132. McLaren 2004, 63.

133. Viola and Barna 2008, 72.

134. Tickle 2008, Emergence, 83; Millnar 2009, 8.

135. Crowder 2006, 306.

136. Stephen Strang, "Good News for Charismatics," Charisma (June 2009): 66.

of charismatic Christians fifty years later.[137] A scant 100 years after its inception, Charismatic Christians – who were later given the label of "renewalists" by the Pew Foundation – grew to collectively account for over a half a billion adherents, making them the second largest Christian group after Roman Catholics.[138] Other sources place the number of charismatics even higher. Adrienne S. Gains states there are "more than 600 million adherents" to the pentecostal-charismatic movement,[139] while Troy Anderson indicates that "there are 640 million Pentecostals and charismatics."[140]

Pentecostals embrace the direct connection between the believer and God via the Holy Spirit, who acts as instructor, counselor, leader, and comforter. In practice, their definitive authority is more experiential in nature than canonical.[141] The pentecostal movement, now more than a century old, has grown to incorporate several denominations that embrace the spiritual gifts of speaking in tongues, healing, and prophesying. In the 1970s, a more general charismatic movement was birthed when Christians in non-pentecostal denominations and congregations began to adopt similar emphases upon the supernatural.[142]

"It is important to realize," says John Crowder, "that the Pentecostal

---

137. Troy Anderson, "Charismatic Renewal Marks 50 Years," Charisma (April 2010): 16.

138. Tickle 2008, Emergence, 84.

139. Adrienne S. Gains, "ORU to Host Global Pentecostal Congress," Charisma (March 2010): 25.

140. Troy Anderson, 2010, 16.

141. Tickle 2008, Emergence, 85.

142. Sarah Pulliam Bailey, "A Voice for Sanity," Christianity Today (November 2009): 44.

denominations were birthed amid division and power plays."[143] Their own denominational squabbling produced more than 200 variations at the peak of their disunity. Much of this disunity resulted from minor, seemingly insignificant differences – one such split occurred over the debate of requiring men to wear neckties – that occurred in tandem with leadership power struggles and selfish ambition.[144]

This proclivity for division has carried forward to the greater charismatic movement that emerged from pentecostalism. C. Peter Wagner notes, "The most lasting results of the charismatic renewal movement were seen, not in the efforts to renew the existing denominations internally, but in the emergence of the independent charismatic churches, congregations that were planted outside of denominational structures."[145] An ecumenical movement was launched in a vigorous effort to bridge denominational divisions and promote unity, but it "did not seem to bear positive fruit."[146]

Historical Synopsis

The followers of Jesus were largely unified for several hundred years until the fifth century and the Council of Chalcedon, which resulted in the first major step of disunity with the departure of Oriental Christianity. Some five centuries later, in 1054, there was the Great Schism, which produced an east-west split of Christianity. A half of millennium later, circa 1517, the Great Reformation resulted in the birth of Protestantism. The Protestant branch of Christianity would go on to spark vociferous division by denomination, ultimately resulting in tens of thousands of disparate bastions of Protestant

---

143. Crowder 2006, 301-302.

144. Ibid.

145. Wagner 2004, 53.

146. Ibid.

theology, but which categorically aligned with one of three camps: the mainline/liberal, the evangelical/conservative, and the pentecostal/charismatic.

The Present Situation

Postmodern scholar Brian McLaren succinctly summarizes the resulting divergent views of these two millennia of disunity: For the Eastern Orthodox, Jesus saves through His incarnation, whereas for the liberal Protestant and Anabaptist (such as the Amish, Mennonite Brethren, and the Church of the Brethren[147]), Jesus saves through His life – that is, His example and His teaching, especially His instructions on ethical behavior. However, it is uniquely the Anabaptists who highlight Jesus' work in forming and growing a community of disciples and followers.[148] For conservative Protestants and Roman Catholics, Jesus saves individuals by dying on the cross and rising from the dead.

Furthermore, conservative Protestants (evangelicals) worship a Jesus who died on the cross and rose from the dead so they can have a one-time salvation experience and go to heaven when they die. Conversely, Roman Catholics have as their focal point the death of Jesus; for them it is the suffering Messiah who they adore and worship.[149] Meanwhile, pentecostals worship a Jesus who provides an ongoing salvation experience through His gift of the Holy Spirit,[150] while liberal Protestants focus on the life of Jesus, His words, and His deeds.[151] Each of these divisions focuses on one aspect of Jesus, dismissing or ignoring other facets, creating division as a result.

"Contemporary Christianity has fallen into the errors of both the Pharisees

---

147. McLaren 2004, 224.

148. Ibid., 69.

149. Ibid., 67.

150. Ibid., 59 & 67.

151. Ibid., 67.

and the Sadducees," assert Viola and Barna. While the Pharisees were guilty of adding "a plethora of man-made rules and traditions" to the Bible, the Sadducees were likewise culpable, albeit in opposite fashion, for their reduction of Scripture to only the Law of Moses and not the entire Old Testament, thereby placing significant limits on their theological understanding. In like manner, today's Christians have constructed a wide array of traditions that either supersede or limit biblical truth while ignoring much New Testament revelation. They "dilute the authority of God's word, either by addition or subtraction."[152] As such, the contemporary church possesses and perpetuates a theological foundation that "has neither a biblical nor a historical right to function as it does."[153] The effective result is the existence of and insistence upon "a great number" of contemporary church practices that are "in conflict with those biblical principles and teachings."[154]

Much of today's Christianity is a direct product of the Reformation. Nevertheless, with that reconfiguration having occurred about 500 years in the past, the next major movement is in the works.[155] Theologian Walter Rauschenbusch was arguably the first to spot this, when in 1907 he declared Western humanity to be in a revolution equal to that of the Reformation.[156] This work will explore these present-day developments (that is, reformation) with this statement in mind. Will this revolution produce greater disunity as historical evidentiary trends suggest, or can increased unity among the followers of Jesus at last be the outcome?

---

152. Viola and Barna 2008, xvii-xviii.

153. Ibid., xx.

154. Ibid., xix.

155. Tickle 2008, Emergence, 27-28.

156. Ibid., 125, referencing Rauschenbusch's Christianity and the Social Crisis in the 21st Century: The Classic That Woke Up the Church.

Research Thesis

Postmodernism, in general, and the resulting new forms of church expressions advocated by postmodern-thinking Christians, specifically, can provide the basis for increased unity in Jesus.

DELIMITATIONS OF THE STUDY

To confine this research within the realms of feasibility and practicality, it will be intentionally delimited in three ways. First, it will be delimited to a Christian perspective. Next, it will exclude any pluralistic considerations. Finally, it will focus on present-day movements promoting unity, saving the substantive investigation of historical ecumenical efforts for subsequent study. Although each of these three topics may be both instructive and enlightening, they will be left for others to consider.

Focus Statements

Three focus statements serve as the overarching structure to this study:

1. To explore what the Bible says about unity for the followers of Jesus.

2. To examine postmodernism's attitudes toward tolerance and acceptance of divergent views.

3. To investigate the reaction of postmodern-thinking Christians to the historical divisions within the church.

TERMINOLOGY

The key terms used throughout this research are listed and defined below.

Ecumenical: from the Greek, meaning "the whole inhabited world," which was later transformed into conveying a longing for Christian unity.[1] It is "of or pertaining to the worldwide Christian church, especially in regard to unity"[2] and "of or relating to the worldwide Christian church, [being] concerned with establishing or promoting unity among churches or religions."[3]

Emergent: in general terms, emergent signifies an arising, be it casually or unexpectedly, a "coming into view or notice," or a "coming into existence."[4] In spiritual terms, it refers to "a movement committed to encouraging the lively pursuit of God and to inviting others into a delightfully terrifying conversation along the way." [5] "Emergent aims to facilitate a conversation among persons committed to faithfully living out the call to participate in the reconciling mission of the biblical God."[6] Brian McLaren and others define emergent as

---

1. Bass 2009, History, 272.

2. The American Heritage Dictionary (Boston, MA: Houghton Mifflin Company: 1985): 438.

1. Bass 2009, History, 272.

2. The American Heritage Dictionary (Boston, MA: Houghton Mifflin Company: 1985): 438.

a conversation and friendship.[7] Emergent is explained in narrative form in McLaren's book *A New Kind of Christian*.[8]

Emergent church/emerging church: the various new forms of church life that arise from the modern twentieth century church,[9] embodying a new reality for church and life within the rapidly burgeoning postmodern culture; they are communities, practicing the ways and intent of Jesus among postmodern cultures.[10] "Emerging churches are missional communities emerging in postmodern culture and consisting of followers of Jesus seeking to be faithful to the orthodox Christian faith in their place and time."[11]

Missional: the recognition of not being "the end users of the gospel" for personal benefit alone, but instead being equipped and sent into the world to love and serve others.[12] "Being missional means that the church sees itself as being missionaries, rather than having a missions department."[13]

Modern: in this study, the "era in Western society following the Enlightenment

---

4. Tony Jones, The New Christians (San Francisco: Jossey-Bass, 2008), xvii.

5. Ibid., 235 citing theologian LeRon Shults.

6. Ibid., 234 citing theologian LeRon Shults.

7. Ibid., 230; The Ooze: Evolving Spirituality, http://www.theooze.com/articles/article.cfm?id=1151 (accessed October 20, 2010).

8. Brian D. McLaren, A New Kind of Christian (San Francisco, CA: Jossey-Bass, 2001), 14-16.

9. Jones 2008, xix.

10. Eddie Gibbs and Ryan Bolger, Emerging Churches (Grand Rapids, MI: Baker Academic, 2005), 44.

and the Industrial Revolution and reflective of the values of those social upheavals;"[14] it began in the fourteenth century with "the creation of secular space, apart from the sacred, which led to a societal fragmentation and the pursuit of order and control."[15] Contrast to postmodern.

Orthodoxy: from the Greek, literally meaning "right" or "correct" doctrine or belief,[16] "straight thinking" or "right opinion." In the context of this work it is used in reference to an understanding of God and associated theological thought, which is the gospel. While some opt to pursue a minimalist approach to the development of their orthodoxy, seeking "the least-common denominator," others view orthodoxy as a historical accumulation of knowledge and thought that is viewed with legal fervor. In this regard, the Pharisees and their expansive Talmud is an historical example that comes to mind. Alternately, might Jesus be an example of the minimalist approach?[17] Contrast orthodoxy to orthopraxy; some advocate that the two must be pursued in tandem.

Orthopraxy: from the Greek; literally, the "right" or "correct" practice;[18] the right practice of the gospel,[19] manifested in a love for God and His creation.[20]

---

11. http://blog.beliefnet.com/jesuscreed/2006/11/bloglossary.html, accessed Oct 20, 2010.

11. http://blog.beliefnet.com/jesuscreed/2006/11/bloglossary.html, accessed Oct 20, 2010.

12. Pagitt 2003, 146.

13. Kimball 2007, 20.

14. Jones 2008, 4.

15. Gibbs 2005, 44.

16. Tickle 2008, Emergence, 131.

Contrast orthopraxy to orthodoxy; some advocate that the two must be pursued in tandem.

Postmodern: that which follows and is reactionary to the modern, manifested by a revival of the old, abandoning divisive differences, and flattening modern hierarchies;[21] it is the point in time when segregated secular space is being questioned, holism is being pursued, and the societal pluralism of Western cultures is being welcomed.[22] This idea of breaking down the secular/spiritual divide is captured in Rob Bell's *Everything Is Spiritual*.[23] Postmodern is not "anti-modern," but more correctly, "after-modern" or "beyond modern." It is more properly viewed as a progression than a revolution.[24] Contrast with modern.

Unity: within the Christian perspective, the accepting and embracing of the individual gifts and specific ministries of those who are different, not requiring conformity in either style or function. However, unity is not the goal; love is. "Unity is just the fruit of love."[25] Out of unity springs revival.[26] The expressed objective of unity is to facilitate the best possible Christian witness (John 17:23, Romans 7:4, 1 Corinthians 10:16, 1 Corinthians 12:27, and Ephesians 4:12).

---

17. McLaren 2004, 23, 32-33, 35.

18. Tickle 2008, Emergence, 130.

19. McLaren 2004, 35.

20. Ibid., 38.

21. Jones 2008, 35.

22. Gibbs 2005, 44.

23. Bell 2005, Everything.

24. Kimball 2003, 57-58; Crowder 2006, 42.

Universal church: the collective worldwide group of people who follow Jesus, also called "the body of Christ"[27] and the "catholic" church (not to be confused with the Roman Catholic Church).

PROCEDURAL OVERVIEW

This work is divided into four subsequent chapters. Chapter 2 is titled "The Biblical Imperative for Unity." It shows that the early Christian church does not divide itself or form denominations; unity is decisively protected and consistently promoted. There are a multitude of biblical references supporting unity, such as those recorded by the disciple John and the apostle Paul's numerous pleas and teachings on the subject to various city churches and the pastors he mentored. Even the Old Testament contains support for unity. Divisions were regarded by early church leaders as sectarian and divisive (1 Corinthians 1:12).[1] It was "biblically unjustifiable," Viola declares.[2] Doug Pagitt adds, "Division is division, no matter how righteous we want to make it sound."[3]

However, the Bible is not without accounts of disunity, starting in Genesis with the tower of Babel and proceeding to early church members who simply cannot get along with one another. Even Paul was not above the fray, as evidenced by his disagreement with Barnabas over young John Mark. Nevertheless, these instances of disunity are both instructive and helpful. Building on this understanding of what the Bible teaches regarding unity and disunity, this chapter will conclude with an overview of the nature of present-day church unity.

---

1. Viola and Barna 2008, 249-250; Viola 2008, 119-120.

2. Viola 2008, 235.

3. Doug Pagitt, A Christianity Worth Believing (San Francisco: Jossey-Bass, 2008), 92.

Chapter 3, "The Role of Postmodernism in Promoting Unity," details that although there is a definitive drift away from modernity towards postmodernity, modernism and postmodernism are at the present coexisting, albeit not always peaceably. At the risk of oversimplification, modernity seeks to exclude; postmodernity seeks to include. In parallel fashion, when Jesus is confronted with exclusivity, He counters it by modeling inclusivity.[4] As such, today's postmodern proclivity for inclusiveness is a worthy emulation of the life of Jesus.[5] It may be from this perspective that Jeff Clark, president of Elim Bible College, quipped, "Jesus might well be considered the ultimate postmodernist."[6] Postmodernism may be the impetus that paves the way for greater church unity.

"The Emergent Movement's Contribution to Unity" is the theme of Chapter 4. As Diana Butler Bass points out, society is currently in transition; it is emerging.[7] This is timely, given that many practices in the modern church are being recognized as mere cultural accommodations for modernism.[8] The emerging movement seeks to dismantle the traditions of the modern church that have become culturally irrelevant, using the kingdom of God (kingdom of

---

4. Gibbs 2005, 119; Rob Bell, Sex God (Grand Rapids, MI: Zondervan, 2007), 101.

5. Ibid., 133.

6. Jeff Clark, "Postmodern World," Charisma (May 2009): 18.

7. Diana Butler Bass, "Emergence Meets Mainline" (podcast, Emergent Village, June 2, 2007, under http://www.emergentvillage.com/podcast/mainline-churches-engage-the-e merging-conversation, accessed December 21, 2009).

8. Gibbs 2005, 19.

heaven[9]) as a focal point in their reconstruction.[10] In doing so, the divergent pasts of disunity are meeting up and moving together towards the future.[11] Emergence is a movement towards increased church unity.

Chapter 5 is the concluding chapter of this work, serving as its capstone. It discusses the implications of the findings, suggesting ways in which these findings can be practically applied, and finally offering recommendations for additional study. No research is ever complete; there is always more to investigate and discover. The enormous topic of universal Christian unity is most certainly no exception. Therefore, this document will conclude with suggestions for further consideration and exploration.

---

9. The phrases "kingdom of God" and "kingdom of heaven" are understood to be synonymous. As rendered in the NIV, Matthew predominately uses "kingdom of heaven," while the other three gospel writers, Mark, Luke, and John, exclusively use "kingdom of God."

10. Gibbs 2005, 46.

11. Ibid., 27, quoting Karen Ward.

Research Assumptions

In conducting this research, five assumptions serve as a foundational guide. The five assumptions are:

1. Christian unity is a significant and worthy pursuit. This is evidenced in that the last thing Jesus did before his arrest and execution was to pray, and the last thing He prayed for was the unity of those who would follow Him in the future. This action in His final hours suggests the overall primacy of unity.

2. What the Bible teaches and says about unity is relevant today. The Bible is both prescriptive and descriptive on this topic; as such, it includes commands to obey and positive examples to follow (as well as negative examples to avoid).

3. Denominationalism is the antithesis of church unity. Those who function within such structures benefit from them and will have an inherent predilection towards maintaining the status quo. This opposition, however, does not detract from the critical importance of unity.

4. Postmodernism is a platform for unity. Two major tenets of postmodernism are acceptance of divergent perspectives and tolerance for those who are different. Unity in Jesus can be easily built upon these two foundational ideals.

5. Those in the emerging church care little about denominational

boundaries and sectarian proclamations; their focus is simply on following Jesus. The emerging church is, therefore, by default inherently moving towards increased church unity.

CHAPTER 2: THE BIBLICAL IMPERATIVE FOR UNITY

The bulk of this chapter addresses the biblical mandate for unity, starting with the Gospel of John (17:21-23, John 11:50-52, John 9:1-7, et al) and then concentrating on what Paul wrote (1 Corinthians 1:10, Philippians 1:27, Romans 16:17, Galatians 5:15, 20, Ephesians 1:10, et al). Other biblical supports for unity will also be considered, such as the "one another" commands (Romans 15:7, Ephesians 5:21, Colossians 3:13, 1 Corinthians 1:10, et al) and the Old Testament (Psalm 133:1-3, 2 Chronicles 30:12, Jeremiah 32:39, Hosea 1:11, et al).

The Bible also contains accounts of disunity (Genesis 11:1-8, Jude 17-19, 3 John 1:9-10, Philippians 4:2, et al), which will be highlighted. Rounding out the discussion will be brief mentions of how ecumenicalism and denominationalism relate to unity.

The chapter outline is as follows:

I. Biblical Support for Unity
II. Disunity
III. A Universal Movement
IV. Chapter Summary

Biblical Support for Unity

The call to unity is found throughout the Bible. The focal point for this is Jesus, where much is recorded in the book of John, with the other gospels also making their contributions. However, it is Paul's numerous letters – especially to the Corinthians – that provide the bulk of the scriptural teaching on unity.

The Gospel of John Speaks of Unity

Not only did Jesus petition the Father for the unity of His followers (John 17:22),[1] but John also recorded a prophecy that unity in Jesus would occur. This transpired after Jesus raised Lazarus from the dead (John 11:1-44).[2] The religious leaders were distressed by this and called a meeting. They realized that their "hands-off" approach to the "problem" of Jesus was not working and they needed to take decisive action (John 11:47-48).[3] Caiaphas the high priest made his unintended prophetic statement (John 11:51)[4] "that it is better for you that one man die for the people than that the whole nation perish" (John 11:50). Beyond Jesus dying for the entire nation, His followers would later scatter throughout the world, to bring all nations "together and make them one" (John 11:52).

---

1. Walvoord 1983, 333-334; McArthur 2005, 1414.

2. Walvoord 1983, 312-313.

3. Ibid., 315.

4. Ibid.

Division: The Antithesis of Unity

Another intriguing passage in John addresses the opposite of unity: division. It arose after Jesus healed a blind man on the Sabbath (John 9:1-7).[5] Some of the Pharisees were so legalistic in their thinking that they could not envision God working on their day of rest, whereas others concluded that such a grand miracle could only originate from a righteous man, that is, someone who was not a sinner (John 9:16).[6] This caused a theological division among the people who witnessed Jesus' miracle.

Much division in the church today finds its cause in this same situation: people, who instead of seeking unification under Jesus, cause dissension and division over theological questions that have no substantive consequence. Their bickering over petty doctrinal issues presents a negative example and is detrimental to their effectual witness, hindering efforts to reach others for Jesus. However, the world can otherwise be attracted to the gospel of Jesus when true Christian unity exists. As a result, disunity emerging from unresolved conflict and broken relationships renders the church's collective witness as ineffectual, with little chance for significant success.[7]

Jesus Foresees Division

Another passage in John's gospel tells of Jesus directly addressing division. He prophetically stated, "They will put you out of the synagogue; in fact, a time is coming when anyone who kills you will think he is offering a service to God" (John 16:2).[8] This repeatedly came true in the two millennia that followed. Not only were followers of Jesus excluded by their fellow believers when disagreements

---

5. Ibid., 307.

6. Ibid., 308.

7. Sande 2005, 47.

8. McArthur 2005, 1409.

occurred, but murder in the name of God was sanctioned as well.[9] Lest any well-intentioned justification for such actions be attempted, Jesus quickly put an exclamation point on the subject, stating directly that those who do such things do not know the Father or Him – that is, Jesus (John 16:3). Concisely stated, those who cause division prove that they don't know God.

In commenting on the Gospel of John, William Barclay notes, "Christians will never organize their churches all in the same way. They will never worship God all in the same way. They will never even all believe precisely the same things. But *Christian unity transcends all these differences and joins men* [humans] *together in love. The cause of* Christian unity...*has been injured and hindered because men loved their own ecclesiastical organizations, their own creeds, their own ritual, more than they loved each other.*"[10]

Inclusion versus Exclusion

A teaching of Jesus related to unity is recorded in the synoptic Gospels (Luke 9:49-50, Mark 9:38-40). Although it centered on the disciple John, John did not include it in his own account of Jesus' life. The disciples were distressed when they witnessed someone outside their group invoking Jesus' name to drive out demons. Ironically, it was John, the apostle known for his love, who informed Jesus.[11] He stated, "We tried to stop him" (Luke 9:49),[12] justifying their actions by asserting that it is "because he is not one of us" (Luke 9:49; Mark 9:38). The disciples' view of the kingdom of God was apparently one of exclusion; it was closed to outsiders. However, Jesus quickly corrected them. First, He commanded them not to stop the man; then He taught them that His movement

---

9. Tickle 2008, Emergence, 46. Disunity has "a bloody history."

10. William Barclay, The Gospel of John, Volume 2 (Westminster Press: Philadelphia, 1975), 285; emphasis added.

11. McArthur 2005, 1296.

12. Walvoord 1983, 231.

was one of inclusion, saying, "For whoever is not against you is for you" (Luke 9:50; Mark 9:40).

In two other gospel accounts, this same concept is slightly reworded when Jesus says, "He who is not with me is against me" (Matthew 12:30; Luke 11:23). The first part of this phrase is alternately rendered as "whoever is not on my side...." (Matthew 12:30, MSG; Luke 11:23, MSG). To reinforce the point, Jesus added that "he who does not gather with me scatters," (Matthew 12:30; Luke 11:23) or more directly, "If you're not helping, you're making things worse" (Matthew 12:30, MSG; Luke 11:23, MSG). Anyone who was with Jesus or "on His side" was to be included. They were part of the kingdom; they were gathering and they were helping. This exemplifies Christian unity. The opposite of gathering is scattering – that is, causing division, which serves to foster disunity.

The Christian church seems to have largely ignored this instruction, acting as though Jesus said, "Whoever does not agree with you is to be excluded." This is evidenced by looking at the historical record of Christianity's 2,000-year movement towards increasing division and polarization, which intensified during the modern era.

Paul's Call for Church Unity

For first-century followers of Jesus, the idea of more than one church in any given city was so foreign to their way of thinking that it never became a consideration, despite conflicts and disagreements. The New Testament referred to churches by the name of the city in which they existed,[13] such as "the church at Jerusalem" (Acts 8:1; 11: 22), "the church in Ephesus" (Revelation 2:1; also Acts 20:17), "the saints in Christ Jesus at Philippi" (Philippians 1:1), and "the church of God in Corinth" (1 Corinthians 1:2; 2 Corinthians 1:1). These city churches were "completely unified,"[14] and they "did not denominate themselves

---

13. Viola 2008, 121 and 129; Dale 2009, 9.

14. Viola 2008, 129.

into separate organizations within the same city,"[15] but included all Christians in that city.[16] The apostle Paul said much on this topic. Acknowledging Paul as "a great apostle of diversity," Diana Butler Bass sees Paul as not promoting "the Christian life as one of uniformity," but as "a community of unity-in-diversity."[17]

The Corinthians Are Called to Unity

Despite this overall picture and practice of unity, the biblical account shows the church in the city of Corinth as encountering threats to unity and struggling with disunity. Paul addressed this topic multiple times in his two epistles to the Corinthians. In his first letter, he begged them to get along and desired "that there be no divisions among [them]"; he wanted them to become "complete," having "the same mind" and "the same judgment" (1 Corinthians 1:10). After he called them "infants in Christ" (1 Corinthians 3:1) and confirmed they were not ready for solid food (1 Corinthians 3:2),[18] he asserted that there was "envying and jealousy and wrangling and *factions* among [them]" which is "unspiritual and of the flesh." He labeled this behavior as that which follows "after a human standard and like mere unchanged men...." (1 Corinthians 3:3, AMP, emphasis added).[19]

Following Paul, Apollos, and Cephas

The context of another situation was the Corinthians aligning themselves with specific apostles and missionaries. Some followed Paul and his teaching and others Apollos, even though the two worked together as a team, albeit with specific

---

15. Ibid., 8 & 43.

16. Ibid., 120.

17. Diana Butler Bass, Christianity for the Rest of Us (New York: HarperOne, 2006), 150.

18. McArthur 2005, 1569.

19. Viola 2008, 120.

specialties (1 Corinthians 3:5-6).[20] Additionally, some were following Cephas (Peter), while others sought to step above the fray (perhaps condescendingly so and certainly exclusively), saying they were following Jesus. Paul rebuked them for their divisions, as they were on the verge of forming four sects: those who followed Paul, those who followed Apollos, those who followed Peter, and those who followed Jesus (1 Corinthians 1:12-13).[21] Paralleling today's denominationalism,[22] the Corinthians undercut God's loving acceptance by excluding others from their self-restrictive fellowships. This undermining of biblical instruction, according to Frank Viola, rendered them and all who follow their example as a sect; that is, being "sectarian"[23] and "inherently divisive."[24] In doing so, the Corinthian church ignored the reality that all who minister and preach need to "have one purpose" and must be "God's fellow workers," pointing others to Jesus (1 Corinthians 3:8-9). After all, it is "only God, who makes things grow" (1 Corinthians 3:7)[25] and "no one can lay any foundation other than the one already laid, which is Jesus Christ" (1 Corinthians 3:11); that is, "Jesus is the only foundation that can be laid."[26]

Communion

Paul continued this theme of unity later on in his letter when he addressed the partaking of the communion meal. He stated, "When you come together

---

20. McArthur 2005, 1569.

21. Ibid., 1565.

22. Dale 2009, 9 & 154.

23. Viola 2008, 250.

24. Ibid., 120-121.

25. Vieira 2006, 139-140.

26. Ibid., 158.

as a church, there are divisions among you, and to some extent I believe it" (1 Corinthians 11:18). He sarcastically asserted that this is because divisions are a means to show who is superior (1 Corinthians 11:19).[27] The implication was that disunity is the consequence of spiritual immaturity and human insecurity.

One Body, Many Parts

In another part of this letter, Paul describes how the Corinthians (and by extension, all followers of Jesus) make up the body of Christ (1 Corinthians 12:12, 27; Ephesians 5:30).[28] In His church, there are many parts, but these parts form *one* body. This body cannot be divided into Jewish and Greek factions or into male and female divisions, but must remain a whole unit if it is to function properly and fully. The composite list of all who are included in the body of Christ consists of Jews, Greeks, slave, free (1 Corinthians 12:13), male, female (Galatians 3:28), circumcised, uncircumcised, barbarian, and Scythian (Colossians 3:11); that is, "uncivilized" (Colossians 3:11). Frank Viola and George Barna note that these followers of Jesus transcended "all natural distinctions and barriers"; they saw themselves as "a new creation, a new humanity, and a new species."[29] Viola adds, "Whenever the church gathers together, its guiding and functioning principle is simply to incarnate Christ."[30]

In considering the body of Christ, "there should be no division, discord, or lack of adaptation" (1 Corinthians 12:25, AMP). The imperative need is to "have a mutual interest in" each other and to "care for one another" (1 Corinthians 12:25, AMP), which is the essence of unity.

An Example to Follow

---

27. McArthur 2005, 1589.

28. Dale 2009, 40; Viola 2008, 117.

29. Viola and Barna, 2008, 150.

30. Viola 2008, 149.

In yet another section of his correspondence, Paul echoed the sentiment of Jesus' prayer in the Garden of Gethsemane. He entreated the Corinthians to do all things "for the glory of God." They were to "not cause anyone to stumble" and must "try to please everybody in every way." Why is this? It is quite simply "so that they may be saved" (1 Corinthians 10:31-33). In commenting on this passage, Ken Sande concludes that followers of Jesus should not see conflicts as problematic, but as opportunities for growth, service, and worship. Interpersonal conflict is not an inconvenience or a chance to assert one's will on others, but as "an opportunity to demonstrate the love and power of God in our lives."[31]

Paul concluded this portion of his teaching with the instruction to "Follow my example, as I follow the example of Christ" (1 Corinthians 10:31-11:1). When this admonition of Paul's is fully followed, the result is Christian convergence, with unity in Jesus as the consequence. This is for the express purpose of the salvation of others.[32]

A Second Letter

Unfortunately, Paul's first letter was apparently insufficient to fully stave off the threat of disunity among the Corinthians, for he addressed the issue again, albeit to a lesser extent, in his second letter to them. Paul encouraged them to jettison their worldly perspective and reminds them that they "are genuinely new creations"[33] in Jesus. Just as Jesus reconciled them to Himself,[34] they likewise have a "ministry of reconciliation" (2 Corinthians 5:16-19)[35] "to be ambassadors

---

31. Sande 2005, 31.

32. Viola 2008, 45.

33. Dale 2009, 44.

34. Christian A. Schwarz, The Threefold Art of Experiencing God (Carol Stream, IL: ChurchSmart Resources, 1999), 8.

35. Sande 2005, 219.

of reconciliation in the world."[36] In addressing this passage, Paul Vieira says that "our message to the world should be one of reconciliation."[37] To reconcile is "to reestablish a close relationship," "to bring oneself to accept," and "to make compatible or consistent."[38] Reconciliation, then, is a push for unity.

Paul writes in his second letter to the Corinthian church, "I am afraid that when I come I may not find you as I want ... I fear that there may be *quarreling*, jealousy, outbursts of anger, *factions*, slander, gossip, arrogance, and *disorder*" (2 Corinthians 12:20, emphasis added). "Gossip," says Ken Sande, "is often both the spark and the fuel for conflict."[39]

Whereas in his first letter Paul wrote that he heard of their disunity (1 Corinthians 11:18), this time he noted only that he feared their lack of unity still existed. This might have been a sign of progress, albeit incremental. As Paul concludes his second epistle, he commands the people of Corinth to "be of one mind, live in peace" (2 Corinthians 13:11). Other translations render this phrase as "be of the same [agreeable] mind one with another; live in peace" (2 Corinthians 13:11, AMP) or "live in harmony and peace" (2 Corinthians 13:11, NLT). Peace is often referred to as unity.[40] Ken Sande notes, "Peace is part of God's character," which should be used to "bring peace to others."[41]

The Philippians Receive Teaching about Unity

The Corinthian church was not the only church Paul felt compelled to write to concerning unity in Jesus. The church in Philippi also received similar

---

36. Jones 208, 78; Sande 2005, 248.

37. Vieira 2006, 238.

38. http://www.thefreedictionary.com/reconciled, accessed April 22, 2010.

39. Sande 2005, 121.

40. Ibid., 46.

41. Ibid., 43.

admonitions in a letter in which Paul encouraged them to "stand firm in one spirit, contending as one man for the faith of the gospel" (Philippians 1:27). This is alternately rendered as "striving side by side and contending with a single mind" (Philippians 1:27, AMP). These words evoke the modern image of an athletic team, working together to attain the common goal of victory. It is rare in sports for a divided team to win; victory requires a unified collective effort. So it is when working to advance the kingdom of God here on earth.

Paul later affirmed that Philippian unity was a cause for his personal joy, seeing them agreeing wholeheartedly, mutually loving each other, and diligently working together with one mind and towards a common purpose (Philippians 2:2),[42] as is appropriate for all who follow Jesus. Furthermore, Paul commanded that the Philippians "do nothing from factional motives" (Philippians 2:3, AMP) and later prohibited them from arguing and disputing (Philippians 2:14)[43] with one another, all of which are causes of division and disunity. Regarding these verses, Ken Sande says that, regardless of the situation, there is the need to "always show respect for the concerns, traditions, limitation, and special needs of others," communicating in a helpful and appropriate manner.[44] Whenever others feel they are being treated critically, conflict is the inevitable result.[45]

The Romans Must Accept One Another

Additionally, Paul exhorted the church in Rome to accept one another.[46] The prime example for doing so was Jesus' acceptance of them. Paul's command was to accept everyone, without exception or limit; it is unconditional (Romans 15:7).

---

42. McArthur 2005, 1715.

43. The NIV and NLT use the word "arguing," NASB uses "disputing."

44. Sande 2005, 147.

45. Ibid., 121.

46. Viola 2008, 118.

He also urged them "to watch out for those who cause divisions." Regarding such people, Paul instructed the church in Rome to "keep away from them" (Romans 16:17) so that they would not be "led astray by a bad example or disruptive behavior."[47]

The Galatians Are Reminded There Is No Division

In his letter to the church in Galatia, Paul issued a reminder that, as a result of their being baptized in Jesus and "clothed" with him, human distinctions have become inconsequential, asserting, "There is neither Jew nor Greek, slave nor free, male nor female"; they "are all one in Christ Jesus" (Galatians 3:26-28).[48] These three dichotomous pairs represent historic divisions over "race, gender, and class," notes Wallis.[49] Tony Dale, Felicity Dale, and George Barna see these inequities eroding, with the church hopefully moving into a time when this ideal can be more fully realized.[50] Specifically regarding the "male nor female" clause, they assert, "It is past time for women's equality"; there is a "need for women to be recognized as equal in value and fully able to play a strategic role in the church."[51]

In addressing a parallel passage in the book of Colossians, Diana Butler Bass notes, "Jesus' earliest followers gathered into culturally diverse congregations.[52] This passage adds "circumcised or uncircumcised" to this list of dichotomous statements (Colossians 3:11). With the comprehensive list of apparent (but false) dualities that included Jew or Greek, slave or free, male or female, circumcised

---

47. Sande 2005, 194.

48. Viola 2008, 150.

49. Jim Wallis, The Great Awakening (New York: HarperCollins Publishers, 2008), 158-159.

50. Dale 2009, 156.

51. Ibid., 162.

52. Bass 2006, 149.

or uncircumcised, it is not a stretch to add modern-day polarized factions to it: liberal or conservative, mainline or evangelical, and Catholic or Protestant. Among such, there is "no difference" (Acts 15:9, AMP; Romans 3:22; and Romans 10:12) or "no distinction" to be made (Acts 15:9; Romans 3:22, NASB; Romans 10:12, NASB; Galatians 3:28, AMP; Colossians 3:11, NASB; and Ephesians 6:9, MSG).[53] Jim Wallis notes that from this emerges the reality of being "still diverse, but equal and reconciled." Despite all the societal forces that could cause division, "we are all the children of God through faith." Wallis concludes by stating that these divisions are "not to hold sway in the new community of Christ."[54] Bass adds that among these variations, "the practice of love bound [them] together," honoring "diversity while, at the same time, fostering harmony and unity."[55]

Furthermore, Paul warned the church in Galatia to avoid "partisan strife" (Galatians 5:15, AMP), "divisions (dissensions)," and a "party spirit (factions, sects with peculiar opinions, heresies)" (Galatians 5:20, AMP). He reminded them "that those who live like this will not inherit the kingdom of God" (Galatians 5:21). This is a harsh and sobering warning for those who divide Jesus' church. Jesus' followers are called to respond to conflict differently than the world does.[56]

The Ephesians Are Instructed in Unity

Paul also addressed unity in his letter to the church in Ephesus, albeit in an instructive, not corrective, manner. First he affirmed that unity in Jesus is God's

---

53. Viola 2008, 150.

54. Wallis 2008, 159.

55. Bass 2006, 149.

56. Sande 2005, 259.

plan (Ephesians 1:10),[57] which we can live in now.[58] Then he reminded them that Jesus is their peace, their "bond of unity and harmony" (Ephesians 2:14, AMP), in order to break down divisions, thereby creating "one new people" (Ephesians 2:15, NLT) – that is, "one new humanity" (Ephesians 2:15, NIV).

Next, he urged them to "make every effort to keep the unity of the Spirit through the bond of peace," noting that "there is one body and one Spirit – just as you were called to one hope," in "one Lord, one faith, one baptism; one God and Father of all" (Ephesians 4:3-6). How can division rightly exist if there is *one* body, *one* Spirit, *one* Lord, *one* faith, *one* baptism, *one* God, and *one* Father?

Lastly, in discussing spiritual gifts, Paul asserted that the ultimate purpose of these gifts is for "works of service" (Ephesians 4:11-12)[59] – that is, for edification,[60] building up the church, God's kingdom[61] to "reach unity in the faith" (Ephesians 4:13)[62] and thereby show the world who Jesus is.[63] Who is supposed to do this? It is "100 percent of the believers," teaches C. Peter Wagner.[64] "Bringing unity and maturity to all," adds John Crowder, is the "ultimate level of success."[65]

---

57. McArthur 2005, 1684.

58. Viola 2008, 109.

59. Grady 2010, Holy Spirit, 102-103; Wagner 2004, 32-33, 64, 96; Kimball 2003, 153.

60. Vieira 2006, 47; Viola 2008, 51.

61. Dale 2009, 150; James Rutz, Mega Shift: Igniting Spiritual Power (Colorado Springs: Empowerment Press, 2005), 64.

62. Wagner 2004, 32-33.

63. Vieira 2006, 49.

Pastoral Instructions to Promote Unity

Paul also addressed unity and the lack thereof in his pastoral letters to Timothy and Titus. He clearly affirmed that church disunity and division is something that his protégés would face. Paul warned Timothy to carefully guard unity in the church that was under his care (2 Timothy 2:14).[66] "Warn them before God against quarreling about words; it is of no value and only ruins those who listen" (2 Timothy 2:14). Other translations render the phrase "quarreling about words" as to "avoid petty controversy over words" (2 Timothy 2:14, AMP), to "stop fighting over words" (2 Timothy 2:14, NLT), and do not "wrangle about words" (2 Timothy 2:14, NASB). Clearly, focusing on theological semantics is a cause of disunity.

To reinforce his warning, Paul further admonished Timothy to remind others to "avoid godless chatter, because those who indulge in it will become more and more ungodly" (2 Timothy 2:16). "Sinful words," notes Ken Sande, "contribute greatly to conflict."[67] James Rutz says we should avoid the trap of trivial talk, suggesting instead that we "favor spiritual topics."[68]

Paul then added, "Don't have anything to do with foolish and stupid arguments, because you know they produce quarrels" (2 Timothy 2:23).[69] Furthermore, Paul warned, "Some will abandon the faith and follow deceiving spirits" (1 Timothy 4:1). Examples of their divisive teaching included a prohibition on marriage and the abstinence from certain kinds of food (1 Timothy 4:3). These "false teachers," says Ken Sande, "propagate values

---

66. McArthur 2005, 1808.

67. Sande 2005, 122.

68. Rutz 2005, 179.

69. Sande 2005, 145.

and philosophies that encourage selfishness and stimulate controversy."[70] In commenting on this passage, John Crowder gives modern day examples, stating, "The church has been in bondage to dress codes, cosmetic laws, and countless other silly issues."[71] A far more serious subject is the divisive quarrelling in today's religious culture over the polarized proclamations regarding homosexuality and abortion. Similarly, on a theological level, teachings on the role and function of the Holy Spirit are likewise discordant.

The same advice was given to Titus. Paul instructed him to "avoid foolish controversies and genealogies and arguments and quarrels about the law," which are "unprofitable and useless" (Titus 3:9). Ken Sande confirms that false teachers promote philosophies and theologies that merely serve to propagate controversy and embolden selfishness; they are a cause of division.[72] Paul gave Titus the sage advice to "warn a divisive person once, and then warn him a second time. After that, have nothing to do with him" (Titus 3:10-11). Clearly, divisiveness is something that cannot be tolerated in the church and must be decisively dealt with. Ken Sande puts a bold exclamation mark on the teaching of unity found throughout these biblical letters, stating, "*Every* Epistle in the New Testament contains a command to live at peace with one another."[73]

The "One Another" Commands Support Unity

Scattered throughout the Bible are fifty-eight commands prescribing how God's children are to treat "one another."[74] Frank Viola calls these "one another"

---

70. Ibid., 51.

71. Crowder 2006, 77.

72. Sande 2005, 51.

73. Ibid.

74. Viola 2008, 88.

exhortations a call for the "corporate responsibility" of Jesus' church.[75] Many of these relate directly to church unity. Obeying these "one another" commands is a sure way to prevent disunity; following them will result in unity.

Consider the numerous "one another" exhortations,[76] such as "accept one another" (Romans 15:7), "submit to one another" (Ephesians 5:21)[77] – that is, a mutual, not hierarchical assent[78] – and "forgive...one another" (Colossians 3:13),[79] which implies confession to one another.[80] Christians are also to "agree with one another" (1 Corinthians 1:10), which Frank Viola says means to "be of one mind."[81] They are also commanded to "live in harmony with one another" (Romans 12:16, 1 Peter 3:8).[82] Furthermore, followers of Jesus are commanded to "serve one another in love" (Galatians 5:13) and to "be patient, bearing with one another in love" (Ephesians 4:2).

Additionally, there are the instructions to "honor one another above yourselves" (Romans 12:10)[83] – that is, to prefer one another in love,[84] "spur one another on toward love and good deeds" (Hebrews 10:24), "show mercy

---

75. Ibid., 185-187.

76. Ibid., 118.

77. Sande 2005, 123.

78. Viola 2008, 199, 211, & 216.

79. Sande 2005, 204-205, 207; Rutz 2005, 161.

80. Simson 2009, 42.

81. Viola 2008, 193.

82. Sande 2005, 250; George Barna, Revolution (Carol Stream, IL: Tyndale House Publishers, 2005), 96-97.

83. Viola 2008, 184; Barna 2005, 96-97.

84. Dale 2009, 6.

and compassion to one another" (Zechariah 7:9), and "clothe yourselves with humility toward one another" (1 Peter 5:5).[85] Next are commands to not break faith with one another (Malachi 2:10), "stop judging one another" (Romans 14:13),[86] not hate one another (Titus 3:3), and "not slander one another" (James 4:11).

However, the most significant "one another" instruction is the oft-repeated command to "love one another" (John 13:34; John 13:35; Romans 13:8; 1 Peter 1:22; 1 John 3:11; 1 John 3:23; 1 John 4:7; 1 John 4:11; 1 John 4:12; 2 John 1:5), which serves to prove that we are truly God's unified family.[87] This is not a suggestion, but a command.[88] "Loving relationships," states Dr. Daniel Egeler, "[are] a mark of discipleship."[89] "As Jesus loves us, we can love one another," teaches Paul Vieira; "[then] the world [will] know we are Jesus' disciples because we love."[90] Specifically stated, as we truly love each other, "the world will know us by that love."[91]

In fully considering what it means to love one another, it is wise to dispense with the contemporary view of love and consider how Paul describes it in his first letter to the church in Corinthians. He writes: "Love is patient, love is kind. It does not envy, it does not boast, it is not proud. It is not rude, it is not self-seeking, it is not easily angered, it keeps no record of wrongs. Love does not delight in evil but rejoices with the truth. It always protects, always trusts, always hopes, always

---

85. Viola 2008, 218, 220.

86. Sande 2005, 150.

87. Viola 2008, 115.

88. Sande 2005, 47.

89. Egeler 2003, 75.

90. Vieira 2006, 128.

91. Barna 2009, 65; Sande 2005, 261.

perseveres" (1 Corinthians 13:4-7). Regarding this passage, Ken Sande says that love "leaves no room for unresolved conflict."[92] To truly show biblical love for one another is to live in unity and harmony, whereas disunity and division are anathema to love; "everything needs to be bathed in love."[93]

The phrase "one another" is alternately rendered as "each other" in some translations.[94] In no instances are limitations or conditions placed on who constitutes "one another" or "each other"; these commands are unconditional. They are all-inclusive, without limit or restriction. Therefore, causing division or disunity in the church of Jesus is done at the disregard of these "one another" commands; there are no special exceptions or extenuating circumstances that allow these instructions to be ignored. "None of us can manage without the others," notes Tony Dale, Felicity Dale, and George Barna. "If one member is not functioning properly, then the entire body of Christ is weaker because of it."[95]

A Building and a People Indicate Unity

Both Paul and Peter used the image of a building to illustrate the unity of Jesus' followers. In his letter to the Ephesians, Paul stated that in Jesus "the whole building is joined together" and that his followers are "being built together" (Ephesians 2:21-22).[96] Using similar imagery, Peter called Jesus' followers "living stones" and said that they are "being built into a spiritual house" (1 Peter 2:4).

---

92. Sande 2005, 48.

93. Dale 2009, 81.

94. The NTL and Amplified versions often use "each other" instead of "one another." Examples include James 4:11 (NLT and AMP), 1 Peter 1:22 (NLT), Romans 13:8 (AMP), John 13:34 (NLT), et al.

95. Barna 2009, 63.

96. Viola 2008, 86-87.

Note that in both cases there is one building, not two or more. Paul says "the whole building," while Peter says "a spiritual house." This is a clear teaching of unity. Of note is the fact that both passages use the verb "being," indicating that unity is an ongoing action. It is not "are built" or "were built" or "have been built" or "will be built" but rather are "being built." This shows that unity is an ongoing effort, not a one-time event from the past or for the future.

In similar fashion to the metaphor of a building, Peter wrote, "You are a chosen people, a royal priesthood, a holy nation" (1 Peter 2:9). Again, note that each reference is a singular image. He did not use plural forms, as in peoples, priesthoods, and nations, but rather a people, a priesthood, and a nation. That is, one people, one priesthood, and one nation. These are all statements of unity, both in identity – people and nation – and in function – priesthood (1 Peter 2:9). This priesthood, in which "every believer"[97] or all believers[98] are included, is "one of the most important concepts of the Kingdom," according to Tony Dale, Felicity Dale, and George Barna.[99] "There is no clergy/laity divide."[100] Today's church needs to elevate and reclaim this important doctrine.[101]

We are one people who are part of one building; we are unified.

Old Testament Affirmation for Unity

The discussion of unity is not, however, limited to the New Testament texts. David also addressed unity in the Psalms. He wrote that it is "good and pleasant" when God's people get along in harmony and "live together in unity" (Psalm

---

97. Ibid., 169.

98. Rutz 2005, 124, 160; Vieira 2006, 55.

99. Dale 2009, 80.

100. Ibid., 179.

101. Kimball 2003, 96.

133:1-3). This "unity," notes Ken Sande, "is not simply the absence of conflict and strife. [It] is the presence of genuine harmony, understanding, and goodwill between people."[102] Although it is sometimes necessary to break away from the church, such as occurred during the Reformation, it is imperative to first try to work out problems from the inside, as did Luther.[103]

Another Old Testament passage records the fact that God gave the nation of Judah the "unity of mind to carry out what the king and his officials had ordered, following the word of the Lord" (2 Chronicles 30:12). This was a unity of purpose and obedience. Other translations render the word "unity" in this verse as "one heart" (2 Chronicles 30:12, AMP, NASB, and NLT). This compelling picture of unity is also used elsewhere in the Old Testament. Both Jeremiah and Ezekiel prophetically proclaimed that God "will give them one heart" (Jeremiah 32:39, NASB; Ezekiel 11:19, NASB). The New Living Translation says, "I will give them one heart and one purpose," which is "to worship me forever" (Jeremiah 32:39, NLT). The Amplified version reads, "I will give them one heart [a new heart] and I will put a new spirit within them" (Ezekiel 11:19, AMP). Compositely, unity is rendered as one purpose, one heart, a new heart, and a new spirit.

Elsewhere in the Old Testament, Hosea prophesied: "The people of Judah and the people of Israel will be reunited" (Hosea 1:11). Likewise, Isaiah foretold: "Aliens will join them" – that is, Israel – "and unite with the house of Jacob" (Isaiah 14:1). Clearly, these prophets –Jeremiah, Ezekiel, Hosea, and Isaiah – were all looking toward the future, to a time of God-ordained unity.

Unity but Not Uniformity

It is critical in this discussion of unity to note the distinction between unity

---

102. Sande 2005, 46.

103. Crowder 2006, 201-202.

and uniformity.[104] For followers of Jesus it is essential that unity be sought in relationship with others. Paul instructed the church in Ephesus to "make every effort to keep the unity of the Spirit through the bond of peace" (Ephesians 4:3). However, there was no insistence upon uniformity.[105]

Unity can exist without uniformity. In fact, the pursuit of unity needs to take place within the context of diversity. For example, a choir can sing in unison (unity and uniformity) or sing in parts (unity within diversity). Alternately, consider a band with different instruments. The ensemble is diversified, but each instrument adds to the music. This of course assumes all are playing together and no rogue performer is playing a different tune (disunity).

Likewise, followers of Jesus need to pursue the common, unified goal of advancing the kingdom of God. Unity is perfected through grace and humility. Theologically, the church should not "major in the minors." If a biblical argument can be made for either side of an issue, then it is a nonissue. The ultimate goal is to attract others with Christian love, not by good preaching or a "right" theology.[106] This is exemplified by the Trinity, notes Frank Viola, which presents a "unified diversity" and a "plurality in oneness."[107] Later on Viola declares, "The Trinity is a communion of coequal persons" –that is, it "is egalitarian."[108] "True unity," adds John Crowder, "is found in diversity."[109]

---

104. Sande 2005, 53.

105. Ibid., 30.

106. Jeff Porte, http://www.thirdreformed.orginside.php?a=PG:207 (accessed August 27, 2008).

107. Viola 2008, 130.

108. Ibid., 296.

109. Crowder 2006, 271.

DISUNITY

Not only does the Bible have much to say about unity, but it also addresses its opposite, disunity. Any discussion of unity necessarily must include disunity, which is also addressed in Scripture – often via negative examples.

Biblical Accounts of Division

As with instruction on unity, the most illuminating biblical examples of disunity are found in the New Testament. Nevertheless, the Old Testament is not without its contribution on the subject.

The Tower of Babel

Unity among humanity was quickly lost in the first book of the Bible, Genesis, at the tower of Babel. There the people's ambition to call attention to themselves resulted in the erection of a grand edifice of self-aggrandizement. God thwarted their arrogant plan when He confused their language, thereby blocking their ability to effectively communicate with each other. At this point, disunity ensued and the people scattered. This halted construction of their egocentric monument (Genesis 11:1-8). Implicitly embedded within this account, however, is cause for optimism. God says, "If as one people speaking the same language" – that is, getting along and functioning as one – "they have begun to do this, then nothing they plan to do will be impossible for them" (Genesis 11:6).

Although God caused this confusion of language, disunity was not His ultimate, final intent. A prophetic reversal of this was given by Micah, who stated that in the last days, many nations will return to God, desiring to know His ways (Micah 4:1-2). God will bring them together again, reuniting them for His purposes.[1] Soong-Chan Rah calls this "a promise of shalom unity" – that is, "a restoration of what was lost in the tower of Babel."[2] He notes that this was partially fulfilled at Pentecost (Acts 2:4), where a single language was restored by the Holy Spirit through the gift of tongues and the multinational gathering of many peoples.[3]

Another prophecy of the "last days," however, will arguably happen first. This was recorded by Jude. He reminded the recipients of his letter about the words of Jesus' apostles, who said, "In the last times there will be scoffers who will follow their own ungodly desires." These men will "divide you"; they will "follow mere natural instincts and do not have the Spirit" (Jude 17-19). Jude implies that those who cause division do so from a selfishly human perspective and not at the behest of God's leading.[4]

Diotrephes Is Divisive

An example of this sort of humanly divisive behavior was leveled at Diotrephes by John in his third epistle. Diotrephes illegitimately took control of the affairs of the church.[5] He slandered and rejected the leaders of the greater church and traveling missionaries and compelled others to do the same. John wrote that Diotrephes "will have nothing to do with us. So if I come, I will call attention to what he is doing, gossiping maliciously about us. Not satisfied with that, he refuses to welcome the brothers. He also stops those who want to do so and puts

---

1. Soong-Chan Rah, The Next Evangelism (Downers Grove, IL: InterVarsity Press, 2009), 122-123.

2. Rah 2009, 206.

3. Ibid., 207.

4. Viola 2008, 120.

5. Ibid., 109.

them out of the church" (3 John 1:9-10). Diotrephes's need to elevate himself and control others produced dissent and division; he caused disunity among followers of Jesus.[6] Referencing this incident, Wolfgang Simson disparagingly calls Diotrephes "the first senior pastor"[7] and a source of leadership-driven division.[8]

Euodia and Syntyche Cause Disunity

Diotrephes was not alone in being singled out for causing disunity. Paul called attention to a disagreement between Euodia and Syntyche, who were embroiled in an unstated conflict. Although both worked diligently and faithfully with Paul to advance the gospel, they were engaged in a dispute that threatened to divide the church in Philippi. Paul begged them to set aside this unnamed issue and "to agree with each other in the Lord" (Philippians 4:2).

Those who follow Jesus must strive to work in harmony and agree with each other; clearly these two were not doing that. To help them settle their differences, Paul focused on what needed to be done to foster an appropriate attitude to the situation and to each other.[9] Paul urged them "to iron out their differences and make up. God doesn't want His children holding grudges" (Philippians 4:2, MSG).

Paul didn't take sides in this issue and didn't even bother to identify the conflict. Moreover, he didn't minimize or downplay their disagreement, nor did he instruct them to become best friends or put on a façade of peace and harmony. What he did tell them was simply that they needed to get along. This is a good example of how to respond to church conflict, which is the source of much

---

6. Ibid., 124.

7. Simson 2009, 70.

8. Ibid., 166.

9. Sande 2005, 84.

disunity.[10]

The Quarreling Corinthians

In his first letter to the Corinthians, Paul confronted another cause of disunity, apparently concerned with leadership personas, or perhaps teaching styles. Frank Viola calls this a "sectarian tendency."[11] In this case, the household of Chloe informed Paul of "quarrels among" the church in Corinth. In polarizing fashion, some aligned themselves with the leadership of Paul, others with Apollos, and still others with Cephas; a fourth group attempted to rise above the fray, simply stating that they "follow Christ" (1 Corinthians 1:11-12). Paul exposed the utter folly of their collective actions by rhetorically asking, "Has Christ been divided into factions" (1 Corinthians 1:13, NLT) or "into parts?" (1 Corinthians 1:13, AMP).[12]

Peter's Hypocrisy

Writing to the church in Galatia, Paul related an account of Peter in Antioch. Peter wrongly segregated himself from eating with Gentiles upon the arrival of some with Jewish backgrounds. Paul called this act "hypocrisy" (Galatians 2:13). Other Jewish followers of Jesus emulated Peter's wrong behavior, also separating themselves. "Even Barnabas," noted Paul "was led astray" (Galatians 2:14). Paul immediately issued a public rebuttal against Peter's inconsistent and hypocritical behavior.[13] Paul then launched into a teaching on grace triumphing over the law (Galatians 2:11-21).

---

10. Resolving church conflict is helpfully addressed in detail in Ken Sande's book, The Peace Maker: A Biblical Guide to Resolving Personal Conflict.

11. Viola 2008, 129-130.

12. Dale 2009, 154.

13. Vieira 2006, 63.

Yet Even Paul Stumbles

However, despite his extensive teaching on unity and his confrontation of disunity, Paul was unfortunately not above stumbling on the issue himself. In the book of Acts, Luke records a "sharp disagreement" (Acts 15:39) that erupted between missionary partners Paul and Barnabas over the suitability of Mark (also known as John or John Mark) journeying with them.[14] In a sad example of division, the once effective ministry duo parted company over this dispute (Acts 15:39). Although this is a distressing event, God did work it out for good (Romans 8:28), with two missionary teams resulting: Barnabas/Mark and Paul/Silas. This allowed them to cover more territory and double the overall ministry (Acts 15:39-40).[15]

Although a reunification between Paul and Barnabas was not directly recorded in the Bible, Paul did show a change in attitude towards Mark. In writing to his protégé Timothy, Paul stated that Mark was "helpful to me in my ministry" (2 Timothy 4:11). This reconciliation between Paul and Mark suggests the possibility of a parallel restoration of the rift between Paul and Barnabas.[16]

Ecumenicalism

A term that seemingly promotes unity is "ecumenical." It comes from a Greek word that means "the whole inhabited world."[17] The dictionary defines ecumenical as "of or pertaining to the worldwide Christian church, especially in regard to unity."[18] Another definition is in close agreement, stating that

---

14. Egeler 2003, 142.

15. Viola 2008, 50.

16. Egeler 2003, 142-143.

17. Bass 2009 History, 271-272.

18. The American Heritage Dictionary, 438.

ecumenical means "of or relating to the worldwide Christian church, [being] concerned with establishing or promoting unity among churches or religions."[19] It is the last two words of this second definition, "or religions," that cause great concern for some, being a key point of controversy regarding the ecumenical movement.

At the dawn of the twentieth century, the meaning of ecumenical morphed into a new connotation, expressing a longing for Christian unity. The birth of this new understanding was likely the historic 1910 Edinburgh Missionary Conference, which advocated church unity to avoid denominational competition and theological confusion in the mission field.[20] This was precisely what Jesus foresaw and prayed against just before His crucifixion, asking that disunity not be an issue that prevents the whole world from believing in Him (John 17:22).

Fast-forward 100 years from the Edinburgh Conference, and Rick Warren notes that missionary conflicts still exist, citing problems in the Philippines between "two major evangelical networks" and conflict in Seoul, South Korea, between charismatics and Presbyterians as two examples.[21] Janeil Owen of the Northwest Haiti Christian Mission also affirms that missionary efforts are often thwarted by disunity. Progress is not limited by a lack of workers, but rather by a "lack of unity."[22] Frank Viola says that the "lack of unity" in the church is quite simply a failure to embrace the headship of Jesus.[23]

---

19. http://www.thefreedictionary.com/ecumenical, accessed July 15, 2009.

20. Bass 2009 History, 271-272.

21. Morgan 2008, 43.

22. Mary Hutchinson, "Ministry Centralizes Haiti Outreaches," Charisma (September 2009): 13.

23. Viola 2008, 193.

Denominationalism

Diana Butler Bass notes that the once singular label of Christian first gave way to secondary identification as Catholic, Protestant, or Orthodox. Further division ensued as practitioners (especially Protestants) adopted even more finely defined labels of their denominations, "aligning themselves with particular doctrines, creeds, and practices" in the process.[24]

According to Frank Viola, the plethora of Protestant denominations – which numbers 42,000[25] – with which Christianity is confronted with today are simply "man-made divisions." These undercut biblical teaching and construct artificial structures that serve to "fragment the body of Christ." Denominationalism was a foreign concept in the early church, which was focused on "the body of Christ alone."[26]

Theology professor John Frame goes so far as to state that the Bible "requires the abolition of denominations."[27] "If we divide over forms of church government or peripheral doctrines," adds Pastor Francis Frangipane, "we will completely miss the true purpose of the church, which is to make disciples of Jesus." He concludes that any focus other than Christ will become a source of

---

24. Bass 2009, History, 295.

25. Ted Olsen, "Go Figure,"
   http://www.christianitytoday.com/ct/2011/april/gofigure-apr11.html,
   (accessed April 2, 2012) and "Status of Global Mission, 2011, in Context of 20th and 21st Centuries,"
   http://www.gordonconwell.edu/resources/documents/StatusOfGlobalMission.pdf, (accessed April 2, 2012).

26. Viola 2008, 125.

27. John M. Frame, Evangelism Reunion (Grand Rapids, MI: Baker, 1991), 30; cited by Viola 2008, 125.

deception.[28]

Viola asserts that people are accepted by God when they repent and follow Jesus. This is the singular requirement of being received into His (Jesus') body – that is, the church. Any requirement beyond this "undercuts the biblical basis for fellowship" and becomes sectarian – that is, a sect. Viola notes that a sect, which can also be translated as "party," "faction," or "heresy," is not part of the church, but is a schism; it is divisive.[29]

With regard to evangelicalism, Philip Yancey notes that among the good he sees in the movement, there is also much disunity. To confirm this, he simply calls attention to the vast number of denominations that fit under the evangelical banner. They "have brought energy to the faith," he notes, "but also division." While evangelicals transform individuals, they often fail to transform society; disunity is implicitly a major cause for their failure.[30] Phyllis Tickle adds that Protestantism (of which evangelicalism is a part) has a "hallmark characteristic of divisiveness."[31] She concludes, "Denominationalism is a disunity in the body of Christ."[32]

---

28. Francis Frangipane, "All We Need Is Jesus," Charisma (November 2009): 53.

29. Viola 2008, 119.

30. Phillip Yancey, "O, Evangelicos!" Christianity Today (December 2009): 65.

31. Tickle 2008, Emergence, 134.

32. Ibid., 46.

A UNIVERSAL MOVEMENT

The early Christian church did not divide itself or form denominations. All first-century Christians belonged to one church. "The unity of the Spirit was well guarded," according to Viola and Barna. "Denominating themselves ('I am of Paul,' 'I am of Peter,' 'I am of Apollos') was regarded as sectarian and divisive."[1]

Jesus called His followers to "a universal movement," asserts Wolfgang Simson, but the result today is "a series of religious corporations with global chains marketing their special brands of Christianity and competing with each other." Because of this, Protestants lost their collective voice in society. Their focus became their respective traditional distinctions, which manifested itself in counterproductive religious infighting. In the course of doing so, they ceased to promote an effective, unified testimony to the world. "Jesus simply never asked people to organize themselves into factions and denominations," Simson concludes.[2]

Avoiding Theologically Homogenous Echo Chambers

In concurrence, Al Hsu notes that a tendency exists to congregate based on doctrinal traditions, worship styles, and church governance practices. All too often, the result is "living in theologically homogenous echo chambers." When diversity is effectively nonexistent, absolute opinions and dogmatic declarations

---

1. Viola and Barna 2008, 249-250; Dale 2009, 154; see 1 Corinthians 1:12.

2. Simson 2009, xx-xxi.

become commonplace. The result is an exacerbation of differences and divergent views.[3] Disagreements like these, adds Mark Galli, will "not go away when we huddle with the like minded."[4]

It is critical that followers of Jesus be unified if there is to be the complete fulfillment of God's intent and purpose for us here on earth, according to C. Peter Wagner. It is obvious that doctrinal differences are a prime contributor to dividing the church, that is, the body of Christ. Although Wagner sees doctrine as becoming less divisive in the coming age, the "spirit of religion is trying to thwart this trend."[5]

There Is Hope

There is, however, hope for a solution to disunity and a reconciliation of division. Frank Viola admits to having been unaware of the extent to which Christian unity can be reasonably realized and practically achieved until he "stepped outside the institutional church" and experienced organic churches that are united around the centrality of Jesus and nothing else.[6] This will be covered in detail in Chapter 4.

---

3. Al Hsu, "Family Ties," Christianity Today (December 2008): 59.

4. Mark Galli, "Reasoning Together," Christianity Today (August 2009): 7.

5. Wagner 2004, 186.

6. Viola 2008, 131.

CHAPTER SUMMARY

The Bible, especially the New Testament, has much to teach and inform regarding the all-critical importance of church unity. Most significant is Jesus' prayer for unity just prior to His crucifixion, as recorded in John 17. This is noteworthy for three reasons. First, Jesus, the Son of God, uttered the call for unity, giving it weight above all else. Second, Jesus communicated this deep desire for the unity of His followers to His heavenly Father in prayer. Third, Jesus demonstrated unity as imperative by making it the focus of His last moments just before His arrest and execution.

Paul, the most prolific of New Testament writers, adds considerable credence to the subject of unity, addressing it in the majority of his letters, occasionally at length. These include his letters to the Corinthian, Philippian, Roman, Galatian, and Ephesian churches, as well as his pastoral letters to Timothy and Titus. Paul's words serve both as instruction and correction.

Although examples of disunity do appear in the biblical text, they are neither normative nor prescriptive. Unfortunately, this is not the case with much of today's Christianity, where division is normal and unity is an aberration.

With an historical, biblical understanding of the critical importance of Christian unity established, the next consideration will be the present age and the contribution postmodernism offers in promoting attitudes of greater unity. However, understanding postmodernity is best accomplished from a foundation of modernity, which must be covered first.

CHAPTER 3: THE ROLE OF POSTMODERNISM IN PROMOTING UNITY

Starting a few decades ago, those in the scientific and philosophy communities began to assert that the modern era was coming to an end. Just as the Middle Ages gave way to modernity, it is now modernity's turn to yield to its successor, postmodernity.[1] Human history is now entering into a new epoch called the postmodern age. Speaking of this move, Southern Baptist leader Reggie McNeal confidently declared that postmodernism is God's "end run around" modernism,[2] adding, "God took a beating in the modern world."[3] Stanley Hauerwas effectively concurs, stating, "Modernity was a theological mistake."[4]

The chapter outline is as follows:

I. What Is Modernity?
II. Postmodern Defined
III. Postmodernism and the Christian Church
IV. A Time of Transition
V. The Millennial Generation

---

1. Bass 2009, History, 214-215.

2. Reggie McNeal, The Present Future (San Francisco: Jossey-Bass, 2003), 5-6.

3. Ibid., 54.

4. Bass 2009, History, 216. Bass cites part of a lecture by Hauerwas that she overheard while attempting to teach her own class in a nearby room.

What Is Modernity?

As discussed earlier, the modern world emerged some 500 years ago.[1] Central to modernity was an underlying understanding of truth as that which can be definitively determined.[2] This was the foundation on which modernity's Age of Enlightenment[3] or Age of Reason[4] sat, domesticating Western thought in the process.[5] As a result, human reasoning was elevated, viewing intellect and logic as superior, superseding the subjectivity of emotion and experience. Modernity asserted that reality could only be tangibly quantified. Therefore, what cannot be observed by the five senses is not real or reliable.[6] This implicit "denial of the supernatural," noted Hwa Yung, "has crippled much of theology."[7]

The Impetus for Modernity

---

1. McNeal 2003, 53.

2. Bass 2009, History, 289.

3. Hwa Yung, "A 21st Century Reformation," Christianity Today (September 2010): 32.

4. Crowder 2006, 39.

5. Yung 2010, 32.

6. Vieira 2006, 77.

7. Yung 2010, 32.

Modernity was ushered in by a convergence of technological advances (primarily the printing press and modern shipbuilding) that moved mankind out of the Dark Ages into the Age of Enlightenment. This modern mindset posited the need to transcend superstitions and the supernatural in favor of the tangible and the comprehensible, the goal of which was a complete demystification of all aspects of life and existence. As such, education replaced religion as the prime elucidator of human understanding and illumination,[8] with spirituality reduced to being "a puzzle to be solved."[9]

For Christianity this modern era marked its beginning with Protestants splitting from Catholics and concluded "with a multitude of schisms and bitter theological arguments between Christians over the tenets of their faith."[10] Some observers view this phenomenon as having reduced faith to nothing more than a semantic quarrel.[11]

The church blindly bought into the ideals of enlightenment, reforming the faith experience into a rational intellectualism[12] and reworking theology to de-emphasize the supernatural elements of faith.[13] At its core, modernity presupposed that a singular religious truth could be ascertained. Therefore, a quest for right thinking was thrust forward with the assumption that ultimately all Christian thought and discussion would converge into a singularly correct set

---

8. McNeal 2003, 53-54.

9. Bass 2009, History, 219.

10. Ibid., History, 289.

11. Ibid., History, 292.

12. Ibid., History, 237-238.

13. Ibid., History, 215.

of beliefs.[14] Diana Butler Bass anecdotally notes that she grew up in this type of homogenous environment – albeit a local one – where everyone "seemed to believe the same things about God and morality."[15]

The Theological Failure of Modernity

Unfortunately, the result of this modernist thrust was not a reunification of increasingly divergent perspectives of faith, but rather a myriad of conflicts between perceived variations of truth, with each faction asserting they were right and all countervailing notions were in error.[16] Instead of answering questions and imparting clarity, modernity ultimately produced greater uncertainty, generated more questions, added spiritual tension, and resulted in unanticipated consequences.[17]

The church was inevitably changed as a consequence of modernity, qualifying pastors by virtue of their education, reducing spirituality to the quantifiable, and adopting the world's educational model as the sole means for spiritual illumination. The Bible itself even became the corporeal focus of religious endeavor, superseding the pursuit of personal intimacy with the God who inspired and is revealed in the Bible. A faith that was rational became the inescapable result.[18] The evangelism movement grew from this mindset, sharing a close connection with and largely gaining its credibility from modernity.[19]

"It is now recognized that much of Western thought has been domesticated

---

14. Ibid. History, 289.

15. Bass 2006, 16.

16. Bass 2009 History, 289.

17. Ibid., 217.

18. McNeal 2003, 54-55.

19. Rah 2009, 121.

by modernity," says Malaysian bishop Hwa Yung.[20] (As a non-Westerner, Yung has an ideal vantage from which to make this observation.) The outcome of modernity's influence on the Christian church, especially in North America, was that faith became reduced to a segmented portion of life, being segregated from other aspects of living, such as vocation, avocation, recreation, and even family. Modern Christians must therefore "go" to church in order to meet their spiritual needs. The effect was that the church in North America compulsively clung to modernity, rendering itself as "more secular than the culture" in which it existed.[21] It is therefore not surprising that author Brian McLaren concisely labeled modernity as "a misdirected project."[22]

Notable exceptions to this shift are the Anabaptists and the Anglicans. Both groups, notes McLaren, withheld "their full allegiance from modernity."[23] Additionally, the African-American church never really bought into the modernism mentality either, as was the case with "many streams of Christianity outside North America."[24]

20. Yung 2010, 32.

21. McNeal 2003, 55-56.

22. McLaren 2004, 230.

23. Ibid., 237.

24. Kimball 2003, 48 (in a sidebar written by Mark Oestreicher).

POSTMODERN DEFINED

In 2003, Dan Kimball wrote that with postmodernism still existing in its formative, development phase, a vantage point is lacking from which to fully define the concept of postmodernism.[1] Even though many changes occurred in the intervening years since Kimball's pronouncement, his insight is no less accurate today than it was then. Even so, postmodernism remains a popular word and a trendy concept. It is an idea that is readily bandied about in today's world, with both societal influences and cultural implications.[2]

Notwithstanding the assertion that it may be premature to accurately define postmodernism, for the purposes of this discussion postmodernity does need to be reasonably articulated. The concept of postmodernity was first used in the field of architecture as a reaction to the uninspired blandness of modern building design.[3] In general terms, that which is postmodern followed and was a reaction to that which is modern.

The precise definition of postmodernity varies greatly from one discipline to another. However, it frequently encompasses a restoration of former styles and methodologies, abandoning differences between various fields of study and leveling organizational structures. Postmodernity, as a reaction to the modern,

---

1. Kimball 2003, 47.

2. Crowder 2006, 37.

3. http://www.thefreedictionary.com/postmodern, accessed November 14, 2010.

often manifests itself as a revival of the old, an abandoning of divisive differences, and a flattening of modern hierarchies.[4] Postmodernity represents a shift away from the Age of Enlightenment and the reason that it espoused, instead moving towards an embrace of understanding and knowing through experience.[5] Postmodern is an era in which segregated secular space is being questioned, holism is being pursued, and societal pluralism in Western culture is being welcomed.[6]

A Spiritual Movement

At the heart of postmodernism is a spiritual movement; in fact, it is a "wildly spiritual" one. Even so, it is incorrect to assume that this move is exclusively Christian. Postmodernity is the response to the predicted nihilism that many once saw as the concluding outcome of modernity. Postmodernism allows for the coexistence of the ambiguity of opposing truths, even to the point of embracing the paradoxical. Consider the portrayal of light in quantum physics (which is foundational to postmodernism). Light exists as both a wave and a particle, even though waves and particles are mutually exclusive phenomena.[7] Interestingly, postmodern generations, influenced by an understanding of quantum physics, are more positively predisposed to accept the concepts of intelligent design and divine intervention than were their modern-thinking predecessors.[8]

Additionally, postmodernism rejects the dichotomy of modernism's secular-sacred dualism, melding the two into one cohesive reality, alternately

---

4. Jones 2008, 35.

5. Bass 2006, 209.

6. Gibbs 2005, 44.

7. McNeal 2003, 56-57.

8. Ibid., 6.

asserting that everything is sacred (spiritual) or that nothing is sacred (spiritual). It is therefore not surprising that many individuals with a postmodern mindset are assuredly spiritual. This allows for a greater consideration of God among the postmodern-minded; even the number of scientists endorsing creationism is on the rise. Postmodern thought advances righteousness, not a merely as a legalistic moral code, but as being in right relationship with others. Brokenness (of which the sacrificial death of Jesus is symbolic) is a unifying factor among postmoderns. Heaven and hell are embraced as viable concepts, as is a better existence in an afterlife. Miracles are expected and common; coincidences are not, as everything is understood as being interconnected. Consider, for example, the global connectedness of the Internet and the communal relationship of quarks in the field of quantum mechanics – nothing and no one exists in isolation.[9]

Not Anti-Modern

It is important to state that postmodern is not "anti-modern," but more correctly "after-modern," or even "beyond modern."[10] In this manner, John Crowder defines postmodernism by invoking a series of other "post-" labels. Postmodern, is therefore, "post-analytical," "post-scientific," "post-conquer," "post-control," and also "post-Protestant." Postmodernity, he adds, does not reject modernity but transcends it. The postmodern mindset is one of searching and exploration; a hunger exists for spiritual reality and a dismissal of analytical religion.[11]

Regardless of how it may be perceived, postmodernism is more a progression than a revolution.[12] Another important characteristic is that postmodernism is

---

9. McNeal 2003, 56-59.

10. Kimball 2003, 57-58; Crowder 2006, 42.

11. Crowder 2006, 42.

12. Kimball 2003, 57-58.

essentially amoral. While this fact horrifies some individuals, it spells opportunity for others, as postmodernism is a canvas on which either good or evil can be painted.[13]

A Shifting Worldview

Although the church is in deep denial about the long-term viability of postmodernism,[14] it is assuredly neither a craze nor a fad. John Crowder concurs with Kimball and others about this on a macro level, but asserts that "trendy" postmodernism within the church likely is a fad, albeit a good one, serving as a wakeup call for the church's lack of relevance to the world around it.[15]

Instead, postmodernism is a profound and significant societal change in the global worldview, where the values and beliefs of modernity are largely rejected in favor of an inviting and evolving new perspective. Modernism espoused a universal worldview where morals and truths were absolute, the individual was elevated, and logical, reasoned thought pervaded. Conversely, postmodernism is the antithesis of modernism, rejecting a singular, universal worldview and absolute truth along with it, elevating community over the individual, while thinking and learning in a nonlinear manner.[16] Regarding the proclivity of postmoderns to reject absolute truth, Barna stated in 1991 that 72 percent of adults between eighteen and twenty-five years old do not believe in absolute truth.[17] In 2005 Barna indicated more than 90 percent of *Christians* do not

---

13. Crowder 2006, 43.

14. McNeal 2003, 58.

15. Crowder 2006, 42-43.

16. Kimball 2003, 49.

17. George Barna, The Barna Report: What Americans Believe (Ventura, CA: Regal, 1991), 83-85.

believe in absolute truth.[18] One might expect the percentage of people who discount absolute truth is even higher today.

Regarding absolute truth, consider, for example, the Heisenberg Uncertainty Principle. The condensed version proposes that one can measure the speed of an object or record its position, but speed and position cannot be simultaneously ascertained with complete accuracy. The more that is known about an object's speed, the less that can be known about its position. This principle progresses on a continuum until the conclusion is reached that the act of observation changes the object observed. The connection between Werner Heisenberg and postmodernity is undeniable. Central to his uncertainty principle is the premise that truth is relative only to the one who perceives it; therefore, the conclusion is posited that absolute truth cannot truly exist.[19] Interestingly, the postmodern rejection of absolute truth is not unconditional. In ironic fashion, postmodern thinkers will in fact accept truth as absolute, providing that it has been scientifically proven.[20]

18. Barna 2005, 32.

19. Tickle 2008, Emergence, 79.

20. Egeler 2003, 55.

POSTMODERNISM AND THE CHRISTIAN CHURCH

Postmoderns deride Christianity primarily because Christians purport to believe in only one singular truth. While not directly rejecting Christianity per se, postmoderns dismiss Christian adherents because their beliefs are proclaimed as absolute and immutable. This perspective is viewed derisively by postmoderns as being intolerant, with Christians trying to unethically foist their narrow set of beliefs on others. Embedded in the postmodern mindset is the inherent conviction that morality is a personal choice, with every one entitled to individually determine what is right and wrong. Postmodern's assert that each person has the right to make his or her own determinations; ergo, no one has the right to be critical or condemning of another's personal choices and conclusions.

Tolerance is postmoderns' ultimate virtue; therefore, proclaiming certain acts to be "sins" is being judgmental or narrow-minded, clinging to an absolute understanding of truth, and forcing one's values upon another. Just as postmodernity rejects modernity's proclivity for scientific rationalism and the pursuit of absolute truth, postmodern adherents are quick to dismiss Christianity on the same grounds.[1]

The preceding notwithstanding, it is important for Christians to proclaim spiritual truth to an increasingly postmodern world. What is even more critical, however, is for those who proclaim Christian truth to actually live it out in their daily actions and interactions. Anything less will render their truth message as nothing more than hypocritical rhetoric, serving to reinforce the postmodern

---

1. Egeler 2003, 58.

rejection of absolute truth and further confirm its embrace of tolerance.[2]

Needed: A New Form of Church Expression

Just as the modern world ushered in a new manifestation of church practice, so too the postmodern world demands a new form of church expression for its constituents.[3] It is incorrect to assume or expect that younger, mostly postmodern generations are merely in a rebellious phase and will one day grow up and return to a modern perspective.[4] Similarly, the North American church, which fundamentally reflects modernity's secular and materialistic mindset,[5] is largely in denial of the postmodern phenomenon, clinging to the untenable belief that the increasingly postmodern culture will one day wake up and return to its fold.[6] Over time, postmodernism will therefore render obsolete many of the goals and activities of today's modern church. Says Reggie McNeal, "Church activity is a poor substitute for genuine spiritual vitality."[7] In response to this trend, he adds that people "are not leaving [the church] because they have lost their faith. They are leaving the church to preserve their faith."[8]

Diana Butler Bass adds, "All organized belief – especially traditional Western religion – has been dislodged as a custodian of national morality and ethics."

---

2. Barna 2005, 42-43; Egeler 2003, 67-68.

3. McNeal 2003, 5.

4. Kimball 2003, 64.

5. McNeal 2003, 6.

6. Kimball 2007, 18.

7. McNeal 2003, 6-7.

8. McNeal 2003, 4; also Dale 2009, 29.

In its stead is the elevated notion of personal, autonomous authority.[9] She concludes that this individual autonomy, coupled with multiculturalism, is serving to quicken "the demise of the Caucasian Protestant-Catholic-Jew religious establishment."[10]

Religious Diversity

Postmodernism is less a reflection of societal advancement than a cultural change; it is not a rejection of the modern ideals of analytical thought and rationality, but a move that transcends them. This allows the pre-modern and even the ancient – which modernism rejected – to be reclaimed, in both the world and in the church.[11] Within this change, talk of religious diversity abounds.[12]

Postmodern thinkers (most of whom are young adults) journey back in time, tapping into a "stream of American theological mysticism." They simultaneously welcome the old and the new, incorporate the innovative with the traditional, and embrace the postmodern and the ancient.[13] With this development, the church is again enjoying the freedom to move in the supernatural (while the world, in parallel fashion, is moving into paganism). For example, there is a resurgence in non-institutional and pre-modern practices of approaching God; there is occurring a renaissance of sorts that is blending the old ways of the church with the new – both miraculously and artistically – providing the opportunity to cease attempts to be merely culturally relevant, but instead to be culturally

---

9. Bass 2004, 24.

10. Ibid., 25.

11. Crowder 2006, 42-43.

12. Bass 2006, 20.

13. Ibid., 210; also Crowder 2006, 37.

leading.[14]

Postmodernity eschews the big, the grand, the powerful, the slick, and the organized.[15] The move from modern to postmodern carries with it a decreasing reliance on centralized hierarchical structures, moving instead towards informal relational and participatory authorities.[16] This reality weighs heavy on the modern church, and especially the megachurch, suggesting that postmoderns will shy away from it, leaving the traditional church increasingly less relevant, with diminished influence and status.[17] The intention of postmodernism, however, is to "recapture the positive values of the past," not to blaze new ground without regard for past knowledge and experience.[18]

Detraditionalization and Retraditioning

Two postmodern terms that are instructive to consider are *detraditionalization* and *retraditioning*. Detraditionalization is the process in which received traditions are not accepted as sources of authority or meaning for life; this is occurring on a micro-level in churches and on a macro-level in contemporary society worldwide.[19]

Correspondingly, retraditioning is "an expression of the theological imagination, as biblical tradition is lived out in community, and is an ancient

---

14. Crowder 2006, 42-43.

15. Kimball 2003, 48 (from a sidebar by Brian McLaren).

16. Thomas L Friedman, The World Is Flat (New York: Farrar, Straus & Giroux, 2005), 45.

17. Kimball 2003, 48 (from a sidebar by Brian McLaren).

18. Clark 2009, 18.

19. Bass 2004, 28-29.

practice of faith that connects Christians to their ancestors."[20] Retraditioning is a response that often transpires when major shifts in Christian thought and practice occur.[21]

Ironically, in actual practice, retraditioning frequently occurs in tandem with detraditionalization.[22] As such, says Bass, "in some Christian circles it has become fashionable to dismiss – or belittle – modern conceptions of Christianity."[23]

The Postmodern Church

Like society as a whole, the church is being profoundly affected by postmodernism, itself transitioning out of modernism whether it wants to or not, morphing into a "postmodern church." To some this implies a welcome move towards evolving into a church that is more *relevant* to its culture, whereas to others this is an unwelcome slide into becoming a church that is *relativistic*, diluting sound and accepted doctrine. While the millennial generation (the demographic to whom postmodernity is most often applied) is likely weary of the postmodernity discussion, baby boomers tend to fear postmodernity as the end of their status quo and all that they hold dear. In truth, asserts John Crowder, postmodernism is merely the setting for the next movement of God.[24]

For example, a decade or more ago, American evangelicalism took four key attributes of postmodernity (overarching metanarrative, deconstructionism, virtual reality, and pluralism) and applied them to a ministry context that

---

20. Ibid., 47.

21. Tickle 2008, Emergence, 28.

22. Bass 2004, 31-32.

23. Bass 2009 History, 215.

24. Crowder 2006, 37.

emphasized community, experience, authenticity, and diversity."[25] This focus resulted in the movement that became known as the emerging or emergent church,[26] which will be addressed in detail in Chapter 4.

A Global Movement

Postmodernity is often understood as a Western construct in response to modernity. It is therefore inferred that postmodernity is the exclusive domain of the Western world, residing within its philosophical framework.[27] The movement towards postmodernism, however, is not unique to the United States or even to the Western world. While the timing varies, the postmodern trend is global. The United Kingdom, Western Europe, Australia, and Canada have already been postmodern for a couple of decades, while the United States is newly postmodern and Latin America is just beginning.[28] Nevertheless, a global movement towards postmodernism is evident and inescapable.

---

25. Rah 2009, 112.

26. Ibid., 109.

27. Ibid., 109.

28. Kimball 2003, 69 (from a sidebar by Mark Oestreicher).

A TIME OF TRANSITION

Although there is a definitive drift away from modernity and towards postmodernity, the two coexist at present, albeit not always peaceably. At the risk of oversimplification, modernity is seen in cultural and societal realms that either require or gravitate towards control, uniformity, and collectivism. Conversely, postmodernity is manifested in those areas that express freedom, individuality, and pluralism.

Modernity seeks to exclude; postmodernity seeks to include. In parallel fashion, when Jesus is confronted with exclusivity, He counters it by modeling inclusivity.[1] As such, today's postmodern proclivity for pluralism and inclusiveness is a worthy emulation of the life of Jesus.[2] It may be from this perspective that Jeff Clark, president of Elim Bible College, declared that "Jesus might well be considered the ultimate postmodernist."[3]

---

1. Gibbs 2005, 119; Bell 2007, Sex, 101.

2. Gibbs 2005, 133.

3. Clark 2009, 18.

THE MILLENNIAL GENERATION

The millennial generation, those born after 1982,[1] are the children of the baby boomers, who were born between 1943 and 1960[2] (though other sources define the time span as 1945 to 1964).[3] Alternately, George Barna calls the millennial generation the "Mosaics" and indicates that they are born between 1984 and 2002.[4] Regardless, this demographic is most likely to be postmodern.[5] To understand this group is to comprehend postmodernity and to garner a glimpse into the future. The millennial generation, following the roadmap of postmodernism, rejects absolute truth, opening the door for a manifesto of tolerance, their preeminent and most esteemed virtue. Notably, they crave connection to others, value authentic, nonsuperficial relationships, and respond when sincere love is offered. Paradoxically, postmoderns are intolerant of people whom they deem "intolerant," such as those who take a stand on moral absolutes. Also interesting is that although a rejection of absolute truth is an often-proclaimed characteristic of postmodernity, it is not absolutely so.[6]

---

1. Egeler 2003, 11.

2. Ibid., 27.

3. http://en.wikipedia.org/wiki/Baby_boomer, accessed March 3, 2011, et al.

4. Barna 2005, 42.

5. Crowder 2006, 37.

6. Egeler 2003, 11; Barna 2005, 42-43.

Dr. Daniel Egeler, in his book *Mentoring Millennials: Shaping the Next Generation*, cites an inspiring list of positive attributes of this burgeoning generation. In comparison to the preceding generation, the Gen-Xers, millennials are more optimistic; have a greater predilection towards achievement; long for order, rules, and clear boundaries; accept authority; and want a cause worthy of their commitment. They have a healthy attitude towards school and education, even to the point of exerting positive peer pressure on the desirability of learning and the importance of academic success. Millennials even do better at communicating with their parents. They are also concerned about declining moral and social values, being less sexually active and more accepting of the traditional values of home, family, and community.[7]

Given this, their openness towards spirituality and God is not surprising; most want to have a closer relationship with Him. Although they reject the label "religious" and avoid the traditional church (with its perceived hypocrisy and baggage), they readily admit to being spiritual. They are cause-oriented, being more committed and more likely than their predecessors to volunteer for movements for which they have passion, providing that the effort is an authentic and genuine one. Environmentalism is a primary example.[8] Another instance of this proclivity, according to Jim Wallis, is that today's youth are increasingly driven by two hungers. One is for spirituality and the other is for social justice.[9] In a postmodern and post-Christian world, these "young activists are searching for something to be the engine that drives their passion for justice and a solid foundation for their lives."[10]

This encouraging list of positive traits is the good news about the quintessentially postmodern millennials. On the other hand, there are also

---

7. Egeler 2003, 32-35.

8. Ibid., 36-38.

9. Wallis 2008, 12.

10. Ibid., 16.

concerns. First, they crave attention, and if they are not recognized for positive behavior, they will easily revert to negative actions in order to achieve it. They inherently sense that any attention is better than no attention; being ignored is the worst possible outcome, resulting in a sad and solitary existence. Such an outcome is perhaps their biggest fear.

Lacking limits and boundaries, millennials flounder and make poor, sometimes life-altering decisions. They are essentially lost, longing for meaning and structure in their lives. Millennials inherently require input and guidance from previous generations, but sadly, this is often lacking.[11] Feeling disconnected from these groups, they become increasingly isolated and lonely, which can draw them into acts of irrational self-destruction. When older adults do try to teach truth to millennials, they often do so by advancing a legalistic list of rules and regulations. This, in and of itself, is insufficient to connect with millennials and therefore fails to inform their thinking.

Millennials need to have an emotional bond with their instructors, be it parents, teachers, or other authorities in order to establish a relational foundation for context and meaning before true learning can take place; a personal connection is clearly required. Additionally, well-meaning parents too often shelter their millennial offspring from the consequences of their actions, leaving them confused and perplexed about right and wrong.[12]

With a rejection of absolute truth, lying becomes an amoral concept, with an inevitable conclusion that the end justifies the means.[13] Additionally, the millennial generation is reluctant to make long-term commitments. They also expect that their vocation will provide not only adequate care and support, but also a sense of community and the satisfaction of their emotional, physical, and

---

11. Egeler 2003, 43-45.

12. Ibid., 46-49.

13. Egeler 2003, 64; Barna 2005, 43.

spiritual needs.[14]

---

14. Egeler 2003, 54.

THE OPPORTUNITIES AFFORDED BY POSTMODERNISM

With postmodernism, the "lines are fuzzy," and in many cases there are not even any lines remaining to be blurred. Contradiction is accepted[1] and paradox is embraced, being viewed as beauty and accepted with a healthy contentment. Although paradoxes can lead to confusion, they are "needed to sustain a deep spiritual life." For the postmodern individual, maintaining a comfortable balance with the paradoxical or contradictory does not pose a problem. With regard to spirituality, postmoderns can seemingly draw from diverse streams of church practice and theology, seeing the underlying unifying essence of God as a common thread.[2]

Many individuals with a modern mindset, especially those in the modern church, fear and even vilify all things postmodern.[3] For Christians with this perspective, it is insightful to realize and acknowledge that modernism introduced many nonbiblical practices and customs into the Christian church and faith.[4] Supporting this assertion, George Barna states: "The Bible neither describes nor promotes the local church as we know it today."[5]

---

1. Kimball 2003, 52.

2. Crowder 2006, 43-45.

3. Kimball 2003, 41-42.

4. Ibid., 49.

5. Barna 2005, 37. The concept is repeated on page 115.

These nonbiblical influences are painfully documented in the astute yet mind-bending book *Pagan Christianity?* This profound and detailed work shows that many practices and foundational elements of today's church and faith are not rooted in New Testament Scripture, but are the result of the influences of the society that surrounded the church at that time. Throughout the past 2,000 years, a consistent pattern is seen in which the world influences the practices of the church, instead of the church influencing the practices of the world.[6]

The unrelenting advance towards postmodernism provides the impetus to rethink historical (and often biblically unsupported) practices, providing the momentum to make much needed changes in how the church of Jesus moves and functions. Regardless of whether it is modern or postmodern, a need exists to make today's church align with a truly biblically based perspective of church practice and faith.[7]

Within the postmodern mindset, truth is migrating from the domain of reason and fact to a new and different realm.[8] The aforementioned proclivity of postmoderns to dismiss moral and ethical absolutes is perhaps the most irksome to the modern theologian. Nonetheless, despite this widespread tendency, virtually all postmodern practitioners agree on *some* moral absolutes, such as the innate wickedness of "excessive violence, murder, or evil like the September 11 tragedy."[9] Therefore, despite claims to the contrary, postmoderns in their actual practice do "truly believe that there is such a thing as truth."[10]

---

6. Frank Viola and George Barna, 2008.

7. Kimball 2003, 49.

8. Bass 2006, 210.

The Weaknesses of Postmodernism

The most apparent weakness of postmodernism with regard to spirituality is an openness to accept and even embrace moral and theological relativism. While this can potentially lead to syncretism and doctrinal compromise, it can also serve to remove the restrictions of institutionalized religious constraints and the persistent proclamation of simplistic answers to complex questions. It is a dichotomous dynamic, possessing much risk with the potential for great reward.

The postmodern church can therefore simply elect to sideline modernity's petty theological squabbles in order to more appropriately focus on God. According to Crowder, they will usher in a "much more spiritual age," providing a vehicle for the prophetic and being more accepting of Christian mysticism. However, unlike medieval mysticism, the postmodern version is more grounded in rational thought, producing a safer and clearer lens through which the divine can be experienced.[1]

Despite the hurdles that postmodernism presents in terms of plurality and multiplicity of perspectives, Dan Kimball is enthusiastic. He says, "I am greatly optimistic. I am finding that emerging generations [that is, postmoderns[2]] really aren't opposed to truth and biblical morals." When postmoderns see Christians who are not dogmatic or reacting out of fear, they are open to dialogue and

---

1. Crowder 2006, 44-45.

2. Tickle 2008, Emergence, 160: Emergents are postmodern.

discussion.[3]

---

3. Barna 2005, 43; Kimball 2003, 76. Although Kimball uses the word "emerging," the context is a discussion of postmodernism. The editorial insertion is made to reflect that reality and to provide a distinction between this and the later discourse on emergence and the emerging church. As noted above, Tickle implicitly supports that substitution (Tickle 2008, Emergence, 160).

GOING FORWARD: THE CONTRIBUTION OF EMERGENCE

Brian McLaren declares, "As we move into the postmodern world, we will look back and see ways in which our modern understandings of the gospel were limited and flawed."[1] Similarly, Dan Kimball asserts the need to reexamine and reconsider modern church ministry assumptions and practices.[2] An effort to form communities that practice the ways and intent of Jesus among postmodern cultures is the intent and focus of the emergent church.[3] This growing effort is called *emergence*.

---

1. Kimball 2008, 9. Brian McLaren wrote this in the second foreword to Dan Kimball's book, The Emerging Church.

2. Kimball 2003, 27.

3. Gibbs 2005, 44.

CHAPTER SUMMARY

Today's world is experiencing a significant transformation, moving away from a modern mindset and toward a postmodern perspective. Despite this inescapable transition, modernism and postmodernism are presently coexisting, albeit amid great tension and with much suspicion. Within modernity exists a penchant towards exclusion, whereas postmodernity espouses the opposite, inclusion. Inclusion is also exemplified by Jesus, rendering postmodernism's proclivity for inclusiveness as a worthy emulation of Jesus and the unity He desires. Therefore, within postmodernism there is the impetus to realize greater church unity. As the principles of postmodernism influence the modern Christian church, the result is the emergence of a new expression of Christianity.

CHAPTER 4: THE EMERGENT MOVEMENT'S CONTRIBUTION TO UNITY

As the global shift from modernism to postmodernism affects the Christian church, one result is a transitioning or an emerging of faith, the result of which is the emergent church.[1] In basic terms, emergence is the reaction by some people of faith in response to postmodernism in the world.[2] This chapter will address the emergent movement and the promise it holds for increased unity among a presently divided church.

A reoccurring theme among this group of emerging Christians is the role and work of the Holy Spirit,[3] who is functionally lacking in the actual practice of many North American Christians.[4] By adopting a balanced, holistic Trinitarian perspective of God, the church will move towards even more unity.[5]

The chapter outline is as follows:

I. Describing Emergence
II. Being Emergent

---

1. Kimball, 2003, 41-44.

2. Jones 2008, 38; Gibbs 2006, 44; Tickle 2008, Emergence, 160.

3. Wagner 2004, 10-11.

4. Jones 2008, 201-202.

5. Viola 2008, 128; Jones 2008, 203; Schwarz 1999, 4.

Describing Emergence

Diana Butler Bass points out that society is currently in a transitional situation, and it is also moving from one space to another; it is emerging.[1] The verb emerge means to rise from, to come forth from obscurity, to become evident, and to come into existence.[2] Parallel to this is the adjective form, emergent, meaning arising casually or unexpectedly; coming into view or notice; coming into existence.[3] In and of themselves, these words are innocuous and devoid of divisiveness and dissention; however, they do invoke a feeling of newness and hopeful expectation.

Once the word emergent is injected into a religious context, however, it tends to produce polarized responses and dogmatic proclamations.[4] Seemingly, many of those pontificating about the emergent movement – whether for or against – appear to be parroting the assertions of others, as opposed to averring thoughts from an informed decision based on reality and truth. As is wisely noted, "Typically any new move of God is opposed by the move that went before it."[5]

In general, it is easier to summarily make sweeping judgments than to seek to

---

1. Bass 2007.

2. http://www.thefreedictionary.com/emerge, accessed November 14, 2009.

3. Jones 2008, xvii.

4. Jones 2008, 55.

5. Dale 2009, 194.

understand from an unfettered and uninfluenced investigation. It is easier still to view all change as bad, rejecting it outright as a matter of principle in order to maintain an unchallenged personal intellectual equilibrium. As such, negativity is a common response to the change the emergent movement calls for. Critics are quick to point out that Jesus does not change: "Jesus Christ is the same yesterday and today and forever" (Hebrews 13:8), and therefore there is no implicit need for churches or their services to change.[6] It is, however, critical to recall that Jesus is all about the transformation (that is, change) of His *followers*. In fact, He urges everyone He encounters (except perhaps children) to change.[7]

Emergent Spirituality

In considering the function of the word emergent in spiritual matters, the phrase "emergent Christianity" often results. (Not only is there an emergent strain within Christianity – both Catholic and Protestant – but also in other faiths, such as Judaism.)[8] Emergent Christianity references "the new forms of Christian faith arising from the old"; it is "the Christianity believed and practiced by emergents."[9]

Parallel to this is the "emergent church," which is "specifically the new forms of church life rising from the modern, American church of the twentieth century."[10] George Barna states, "We are living in the midst of a silent revolution of faith. Millions of Christians throughout the world are leaving the old, accepted ways of

---

6. Bass 2006, 241.

7. Ibid., 24.

8. http://synagogue3000.org.

9. Jones 2008, xix.

10. Ibid., xix.

'doing church.'"[11] They "are not called to *go* to church," but "to *be* the church";[12] in fact, their passions compel them "to *be* the church."[13]

Emergence is both a timely and an imperative move given that many of the common practices in the modern church are little more than accommodations for a culture – the modern culture – that is essentially and fundamentally disappearing.[14] Therefore, in the spiritual context, this movement of emergence seeks to dismantle the customs and practices of the modern church that have become culturally irrelevant, using the kingdom of God (kingdom of heaven[15]) as a focal point in their reconstruction;[16] this is alternately viewed as a religious deinstitutionalization.[17] Sociologist Christian Smith notes that if the church does not offer the emerging generation something "genuinely different," they will

---

11. Viola and Barna 2008, xxv; Barna 2005, 61.

12. Barna 2005, 39; Barna's emphasis.

13. Barna 2005, 125; Barna's emphasis.

14. Gibbs 2005, 19.

15. The phrases "kingdom of God" and "kingdom of heaven" are understood to be synonymous. As rendered in the NIV, Matthew predominately uses "kingdom of heaven," while the other three gospel writers, Mark, Luke, and John, exclusively use "kingdom of God."

15. The phrases "kingdom of God" and "kingdom of heaven" are understood to be synonymous. As rendered in the NIV, Matthew predominately uses "kingdom of heaven," while the other three gospel writers, Mark, Luke, and John, exclusively use "kingdom of God."

16. Gibbs 2005, 46.

17. Miller 2010, 2, citing Gary Laderman, professor of American religious history at Emory University.

quickly dismiss it.[18]

The hopeful and anticipated result of emergent Christianity and the emergent church is a return to "vintage Christianity,"[19] when followers of Jesus met in homes, but from which today's church has greatly strayed.[20] This move is expected to produce an explosive spiritual growth, both qualitatively and quantitatively, paralleling that of the early church[21] but not necessarily emulating it.[22] In this type of New-Testament-style church reside those who desire and know how to experience and express God corporately "without any human officiation." As such, they organically function as a church collective, that is the local body of Christ, even when their church planter moves on, leaving them on their own."[23]

A Response to Modernity

In this discussion, the word "modern" hints at the root of the controversy. The antithesis of modern is postmodern. In the spiritual sphere, emergence can be seen as the not unexpected birth[24] that results from reconciling the confrontation between an increasingly postmodern society and the institutional (that is,

---

18. Katelyn Beaty, "Lost in Translation," Christianity Today (October 2009): 37, interviewing Christian Smith.

19. Kimball 2003, 29 and 36.

20. Kimball 2007, 86.

21. Kimball 2003, 29 and 36.

22. Crowder 2006, 257-258.

23. Viola and Barna 2008, 234.

24. Jones 2008, 38.

modern or, according to Kent Smith, legacy[25]) church.[26] At their core, emergents are decidedly a movement arising from a foundation of postmodernity.[27]

The fault of modernity was that it essentially removed the church from mainstream society, relegating it to the inconsequential margins. The church's response to this was a further retreat from that domain, becoming willingly (or fearfully) segregated. As a result, an unprecedented and unwarranted division of human existence ensued, causing a separation into secular and spiritual spheres of subsistence.[28] Within this context it was easier to define what is sacred and what is not. Therefore, the "spiritual" became those things done at church or in holy places, with the "secular" existing as all else. However, for nonmodern religions (both the postmodern and the pre-modern), this spiritual/secular divide is both artificial and unnecessary. The nonmodern Christian adherent lives life with a holistic mindset, seeing all facets of existence as sacred.[29]

For the modern Christian, there is an intrinsic desire to be able to provide a pat theological answer for every confronting question, issue, and challenge. This tendency lacks spiritual depth and experiential substance, serving merely to simplify the spiritual and "dumb down" the divine. In sharp contrast, the postmodern mindset has an inherent yearning for a substantive supernatural experience that is intimate, real, and relevant. In doing so, postmoderns eschew religiosity and untenable theological theory in favor of a tangible supernatural experience with an existent and emotive God.[30]

---

25. Dale 2009, 28.

26. Beliefnet, http://blog.beliefnet.com/jesuscreed/2006/11/bloglossary.html (accessed October 20, 2010); Gibbs 2006, 44.

27. Tickle 2008, Emergence, 160.

28. Gibbs 2005, 87 & 118.

29. Ibid., 217-218.

30. Crowder 2006, 365-366.

One outcome of modernity was "the denial of the supernatural." This had a crippling effect on theology, which led to "at least two serious consequences," according to Hwa Yung. One was a failure to adequately address the demonic and the other was neglecting to include "the 'signs and wonders' of the Holy Spirit into [one's] theological framework."[31] It is no wonder, then, that "little of modern Christianity requires Heaven's intervention."[32] With modernity on the wane, "the world is waiting to see true spiritual power." As a result, "illustrated sermons, great music, or friendly services" are no longer satisfying[33] to an increasingly postmodern society.

In modernity, most Christians placed emphasis on the Bible as being authoritative, inerrant, infallible, objective, absolute, and literal. In contrast, Brian McLaren implicitly advocates that the purpose of the Bible is simply "to equip God's people for good works." Over time, when this has been followed, Christianity flourished; conversely, when the Bible has been used as a weapon to threaten, intimidate, and diminish others, Christianity has languished. McLaren cites Paul's instruction to Timothy and the book of Proverbs as books that affirm the intended purpose of the Bible; other texts include Psalm 119 and Deuteronomy 29:29.[34]

Toward this end, the Bible needs to be reclaimed as narrative,[35] letting the text teach and elucidate God's story, will, and dream for His followers.[36] Tickle confidently asserts, "Emergence is the whole narrative."[37] This will be detailed in

---

31. Yung 2010, 32.

32. Kris Vallotton and Bill Johnson, The Supernatural Ways of Royalty (Shippensburg, PA: Destiny Publishers Inc., 2006), 152.

33. Vallotton 2006, 146.

34. McLaren 2004, 182-183.

36. Ibid., 190.

the following sections.

The Early Days of Emergence

One of the early participants in the emergent movement (circa 1997[38]) was Tony Jones. He gives an insightful, cogent, insider's view of it in his book *The New Christians: Dispatches from the Emergent Frontier*, where he lists twenty characteristics of the emergent church, which he calls "dispatches." In his travels as a sought-after speaker, he repeatedly encounters those he labels "emergents" who are seeking the emergence of a new form of church, who are yearning for a new and different way of practicing Christianity. Intriguingly, these new ways are often derived from the old, be it the pre-modern or even the ancient.[39] In his book, Jones's fourth and tenth "dispatch" both refer to the conversational aspect of emergence. It is not surprising that the emergent movement is sometimes called the emergent conversation.[40] In seemingly complementary fashion, Bass notes that "conversation is pilgrimage."[41]

While rejecting "lifeless and unexplained ritual,"[42] Dan Kimball, another early emergent participant, believes that emergents actually appreciate historical worship rituals once they are understood and practiced in a meaningful and life-giving manner.[43] Similarly, church historian and author Diana Butler Bass sees a renewed interest among some of the younger generation for a more

---

38. Jones 2008, 41.

39. Ibid., xvi & 41.

40. Ibid., 41 and 111; see Appendix A for details. See also Tickle 2008, Emergence, 153.

41. Bass 2006, 65.

42. Kimball 2007, 76.

43. Ibid., 92.

liturgical worship experience.[44] In doing so, they are intentionally pursuing "a variety of tradition-specific forms" – a phrase she employs to summarize Henri Nouwen's teaching to live in "the wide stream of Christian traditions, from desert monasticism to Orthodox icons, from medieval mysticisms to Latin American liberation theology."[45] In similar fashion, Horace Bushnell advocates a connecting of "the Christian future with the Christian past." From this, a more unified universal Christian church will emerge.[46]

The mainline congregations (think "name brand" – a label used to concisely communicate "mainline" to the religiously unversed[47]) that Bass visits and converses with are emerging. They are recombining elements of tradition, practice, and wisdom into their pilgrimage, and along the way they eschew modern religious structures in order to become a more authentic church.[48] This suggests an integral element of emergence is the constructive conversation of people seeking to facilitate productive dialogue among those desiring to faithfully live out and participate in a biblical faith that is both reconciling and missional. Kimball says, "Being missional means that the church sees itself as being missionaries, rather than having a missions department, and that we see ourselves as missionaries right where we live."[49]

The Pursuit of God
As being both missional and a conversation, emergence is an effort and

---

44. Bass 2004, 13.

45. Ibid., 19; Bass 2009 History, 286.

46. Horace Bushnell, Building Eras in Religion (Charleston, SC: Nabu Press, 2010), 438. This teaching is circa 1848.

47. Bass 2007.

48. Bass 2006, 253-254.

49. Kimball 2007, 20.

movement that encourages "the lively pursuit of God," notes Tony Jones, while "inviting others into a delightfully, terrifying conversation along the way."[50] Similarly, Doug Pagitt states that dialogue is a "lost art in Christianity." Over time the early church model has given way to today's "speaker/audience model," and the method of dialogue as a spiritual formation facilitator has been largely lost. He notes that some people learn by talking; when they merely listen to a sermon or teaching, sans dialogue, there is no time to process the ideas. "One-way communication leaves people frustrated."[51]

In addition to Jones, another early practitioner of the emergent conversation is Dan Kimble, author of the 2003 book *The Emerging Church: Vintage Christianity for New Generations*. It was one of the first books to comprehensively address this burgeoning subject. In the foreword, Rick Warren hails Kimble's work as a "detailed example of what a purpose-driven church can look like in a postmodern world," explaining how the church can be appropriately manifested for those who think and feel in postmodern terms. Warren concludes his opening remarks by affirming the need for churches that are mutually postmodern and purpose-driven.[52] Emergence seeks to do just that, embodying a new reality for church and life within the rapidly evolving postmodern culture.[53]

Although the phrase "emerging church" is used herein to reflect a widespread, virtually worldwide phenomenon and not a specific congregation, Bass notes that individual assemblies can also emerge as a group. "They are being formed around clusters of Christian practices – not out of any denominational program or church-growth strategy." They are undergoing a shift to "practice-oriented

---

50. Jones 2008, 234.

51. Pagitt 2003, 89-90.

52. Kimball 2003, 7-8.

53. Gibbs 2005, 44.

spirituality."[54]

Not Just a Fad

With 30 percent of Americans asserting that they are spiritual but not religious,[55] emergence becomes more than a flickering fad,[56] a rebellious craze, or a short-term phenomenon. The established church must not just patiently wait for emergent adherents to return to the fold and re-embrace modernity's behaviors and beliefs. The harsh reality is that, as a group, the baby boom generation will be the last to find a home in the modern church, notes Eddie Gibbs and Ryan Bolger.[57] Tickle also asserts that this is not a generational issue and that these expatriates will not return.[58]

Paul Vieira notes that it is the children of these baby boomers, Generation X, who largely comprise the emerging generation. Vieira, himself a member of Gen-X, focuses the attention of his writing on this generation. Although he doesn't address it, Generation Y or the Millennials – who follow Gen-X – are even more prone to embrace the emergent movement.[59]

Many of this younger generation – those with a postmodern predisposition – have an innate and inherent desire for a fresh and different kind of church experience, departing from their upbringing and experience as children. In their

---

54. Bass 2004, 64.

55. Lisa Miller, "We are All Hindus Now," Newsweek, August 31, 2009, under http://www.newsweek.com/id/212155 (accessed January 7, 2010), 2; Tickle 2008, Emergence, 91; Bass 2009, History, 281.

56. Tullian Tchividjian, Unfashionable (Colorado Springs: Multnomah Books, 2009), 15.

57. Gibbs 2005, 21.

58. Tickle 2008, Emergence, 135.

59. Vieira 2006, 69.

angst, however, most are careful to not reject the God who made the church, but merely what has become the institution of the church.[60] "The purpose of institutions," notes Rick Warren, "is to preserve the innovation of the previous generation"; this ensures continuity, but it does not allow for the creation of new things.[61]

Intuitively, the emerging demographic understands this and knows where they are headed.[62] "Younger generations don't want trendy engagement from the church; in fact, they're suspicious of it," writes Tullian Tchividjian in his book *Unfashionable*. "Instead they want truthful engagement with historical and theological solidity that enables meaningful interaction with transcendent reality. They want desperately to invest their life in something worth dying for, not some here-today-gone-tomorrow fad."[63]

In general terms, it is the emerging church for which they yearn. Phyllis Tickle places the historical significance of the emergent church into its proper perspective in terms of both scope and scale by equating it to the Protestant Reformation. This, she asserts, is something of which she is sure; it is not a wish, a hope, a belief, or a hyperbolic statement.[64] To reinforce this declaration, she bestows on it the moniker of the "Great Emergence" and authored an insightful book by that name that elucidates this assertion. Her advocacy of what she

---

60. Josh Loveless, "Church Mutiny," Relevant (November/December 2009): 62.

61. Morgan 200, 45.

62. Loveless 2009, 62.

63. Tchividjian 2009, 15; also in multiple online posts, including http://www.christianity.com/home/christian%20living%20features/11597 521/print/, accessed 3/5/2010.

64. McLaren 2004, 12. Phyllis Tickle stated this in her foreword to McLaren's book.

calls the "Great Emergence" transcends any general discussion of emergence.[65] In doing so, Tickle asserts, "The religious expression or result of the Great Emergence is a new configuration of Christianity; [it] is fundamentally a body of people, a conversation."[66] The Great Emergence will be covered in greater detail later on in this chapter.

Despite this discourse, there is not a singular formula or ideal pattern for the emerging church; in reality, emergence is more mindset than model.[67] Rethinking church for the emerging generations means reconsidering virtually everything that the modern church does.[68] As such, emergent churches become faith communities, intentionally endeavoring to practice the ways and follow the actions of Jesus as applicable within an increasingly postmodern culture.[69]

Responding to the Modern Culture

"American Christianity has acquiesced to the materialistic values of American society and is no longer distinguishable in its values and norms from the excessive materialism of American society,"[70] declares professor and pastor Soong-Chan Rah. He notes that the North America church is blindly following the materialistic and consumeristic worldview of its culture and the greater society in which it exists; it has been taken captive,[71] willingly and enthusiastically

---

65. Tickle 2008, Emergence, 120.

66. Ibid., 104.

67. Kimball 2003, 14.

68. Ibid., 37.

69. Gibbs 2005, 44.

70. Rah 2009, 51.

71. Ibid., 47.

adapting to this American ethos.[72] The religious result of this consumer mindset is the phenomenon of "church shopping" – which he blames on American evangelism – where the church is commonly viewed as a commodity to be examined, procured, and consumed. If one church fails to meet an individual's needs or provide acceptable value, it is summarily rejected and an alternate church is quickly sought to replace it.[73] This trend is most exemplified by the megachurch phenomenon, which, although shrewdly reaching the masses in a culture-centric manner, is inadvertently advancing Christian consumerism to the level of peddling the gospel as a commodity product.[74]

Many of the emergent movement's pastors, Rah states, are "emerging out of a disgruntlement with baby boomer evangelism."[75] Central to this, Rah notes, is that the church in America is following the "Western, white culture" and focusing "its theology and ecclesiology [on] the primacy of the individual."[76] As such, an undue emphasis on individualism and personalization is propagated by the American church, which parallels the culture's narcissism instead of embracing "the redemptive power of the gospel message."[77] This theological overemphasis on the individual, as practiced by evangelicals, allows for the conclusion that ideals such as social justice and racial reconciliation are trivial concerns, serving as mere distractions from the primary work of personal evangelism.[78]

---

72. Ibid., 49.

73. Ibid., 55.

74. Adam S. McHugh, Introverts in the Church (Downers Grove, IL: InterVarsity Press, 2009), 26.

75. Rah 2009, 125.

76. Ibid., 29.

77. Ibid., 33.

78. Ibid., 41.

However, rather than blame evangelicals for a distorted elevation of the individual, J. Lee Grady connects the roots of individualism to a couple of centuries of modernity's rule. The result is the exaltation of the individual, particularly in the American context, to a level he labels as "hyper-individualism," calling it the "omnipresent norm, the oxygen we breathe."[79]

Agreeing that this elevation of the individual is unwarranted and unwise, Rah notes that most of the books in the Bible have a community focus, not an individual one.[80] In a confirming manner, the prayer that Jesus taught to His followers uses the inclusive plural pronouns of *our* and *us* – "Our Father," "give us," "our...bread," "forgive us," "lead us," and "deliver us" – as opposed to the individual emphasis of *me* and *my* (Matthew 6:11-13).

One key attribute of the emergent church in addressing this tendency is a conscious shift from the current consumerism mindset – as unwittingly propagated by the modern church in the United States – to having a missional orientation; that is, to be mission-minded both in word and with action.[81] Today's modern church is in dire need of "a missional fix," states Reggie McNeal.[82] It is not surprising then that Wesley Granberg-Michaelson of the Reformed Church of America sees the real Protestant divide today not as between liberal and evangelical church orientations, but rather one of settled churches versus missional churches.[83]

In making this missional move, emergents seek to redefine the practical reality of church life springing from a truly scriptural basis, teaching how the church

---

79. Grady 2010, Holy Spirit, 13.

80. Rah 2009, 33.

81. Kimball 2003, 95.

82. McNeal 2003, 10.

83. Wallis 2008, 15.

of Jesus fits into and is consistent with the biblical narrative.[84] As research professor and theologian David F. Wells quips, "Let's have a robust recovery of biblical Christianity."[85] Author and house church advocate James Rutz is more even trenchant in this regard, noting that "almost everything in today's church is foreign to the Bible," with the "traditional, Western, institutional church" being built on "a foundation of digressions from Scripture."[86] In like terms, Wolfgang Simson advocates the careful contemplation of "biblical principles rather than cultural pragmatism." Furthermore, he promotes faith over formula, people above program, and simplicity transcending superficiality.[87]

---

84. Kimball 2003, 95.

85. This quote is from a blog by Dave Englund and attributed to "David Wells" (http://www.daveenglund.name/dblog/2006/08/come-now-and-le.html, dated August 30, 2006 and accessed November 17, 2008). In contacting the most promising source, David F. Wells, senior research professor at Gordon-Conwell Theological Seminary, he humbly stated that he might have said this in one of the many interviews he grants; regardless, he affirmed that he heartily concurs with it (communicated via email January 9, 2009).

86. Rutz 2005, 212.

87. Simson 2009, vii-viii.

BEING EMERGENT

What is it like to be emergent? Knowing *about* emergence is not sufficient to fully comprehend its scope and significance. With its heavy influences, courtesy of postmodernity, emergence is manifested in several distinct ways. While not all-inclusive, the following serves to elucidate some of emergence's central characteristic traits.

Embracing the Paradox

The Bible is filled with many paradoxes, such as losing one's life to save it (Luke 9:24; Luke 17:33; Matthew 16:25; Mark 8:35), being last to be first (Matthew 19:30, 20:16, Mark 9:35, 10:31, Luke 10:13, 13: 30), and serving in order to lead (Luke 22:26, Matthew 26:10, Mark 10:43), to list a few. Similarly, Christian theology emanating from biblical text is not without its "beautiful" paradoxes ("beautiful" is the word used by Episcopal priest Reverend Alice Connor regarding paradoxes in general and the Trinity specifically).[1] Perhaps the two most perplexing Christian paradoxes are that God is three persons in one and that Jesus is both fully human and fully divine.[2]

In like manner, emergence abounds in and even embraces the paradoxical. Jones says in emergent Dispatch 14, "Emergents embrace paradox, especially

---

1. Bass 2006, 208.

2. Jones 2008, 162-169.

those that are core components of the Christian story."[3] Interestingly, Martin Luther also was delighted by the spiritual paradox, insisting "that the tension could be resolved through love."[4] Emergents are not afraid of paradox and they even revel in it, recognizing and accepting the ubiquity of it.[5]

Brian McLaren states that rather than attempting to resolve the paradoxical, emergents live with paradox. He advocates that the right course is to move beyond it, to transcend it.[6] Similarly, Barna says, "Being a revolutionary is all about living life as a paradox."[7] Although subtle differences exist, both authors essentially use "emergent" and "revolutionary" in their respective works to refer to the same concept.

Diana Butler Bass calls this phenomenon orthoparadox. It is living into a grand tension; it is what emergents and their communities can bring to one another; it is being rooted in tradition, yet simultaneously being open to new and innovative forms of expression.[8]

The aforementioned intersection of theology and practice is but one such paradoxical challenge. While part of Christendom places emphasis on having the right doctrine (that is, their orthodoxy[9]), opposing factions embrace the application of faith (that is, right practice or their orthopraxy).[10] This tension is not new. Nearly two thousand years ago, James said, "Show me your faith without

---

3. Jones 2008, 155 & 163.

4. Bass 2009, History, 182.

5. Tickle 2008, Emergence, 160.

6. McLaren 2004, 295.

7. Barna 2005, 84.

8. Bass 2007.

9. Jones 2008, 148-155.

10. Bass 2007.

deeds, and I will show you my faith by what I do" (James 2:18). Emergents, however, don't make a decisive determination in this debate between right belief and right action; instead, they pursue both equally.[11] They embrace it as paradox and then move beyond it.

The Emergent Perspective on Politics

Another puzzling area in the world of emergence is the acceptance (or perhaps, the disregard) of the right and the left, both religiously and politically. Tony Jones states in emergent Dispatch 2 that "emergents reject the politics and theologies of left versus right."[12] Those factions are commonly labeled as the mainline left and the evangelical right. Emergents instead opt for the radical center[13] or what Jim Wallis calls "the moral center." He states that the "People I meet across the country are yearning for a moral center for our public life and political discourse, with a fundamental emphasis on the common good."[14]

The political right (that is to say, Republicans) is criticized for manipulating religion,[15] whereas the political left (that is to say, Democrats) receives criticism for being irreligious and secular.[16] Amid this polarized dichotomy is the sagacious reminder that Jesus teaches to "give to Caesar what is Caesar's, and to God what is God's" (Matthew 22:21; Mark 12:17; Luke 20:25).

Concerning this political/religious schism, Jim Wallis is optimistic. In his travels, he meets "new evangelicals" who are discarding partisanship and

---

11. Tickle 2008, Emergence, 147-148.

12. Jones 2008, 20.

13. Bass 2006, 271.

14. Wallis 2008, 81.

15. Bass 2006, 267.

16. Bass 2006, 269.

parochialism in favor of Jesus. Furthermore, Protestants are returning to their roots, reconnecting social justice with evangelistic activity, while Catholics are reconnecting with the social aspect of their tradition and a faith that is more personal.[17]

Jettisoned in the process of shunning the aforementioned Christian consumerism and embracing truly biblical practices is the rejection of a blind, unexamined, capitulation to the whims of secular culture, be it in the form of polarizing politics or in social activism.[18] Wallis notes that many adherents in the evangelical and pentecostal camps are abandoning their past "religious right" mentality, while intentionally remaining true to their desire to integrate their faith with their life in the world, (possibly becoming a political tipping point in the process).[19]

As this transition occurs, it is not surprising that the emergent church collectively concurs, working to intentionally create a community that transverses political positions, as well as theological tenets.[20] Concerning political engagement, the U.S. Catholic bishops advanced four principles, which likely resonate with the emergent mindset. These guidelines are to be 1) "political but not partisan," 2) "principled but not ideological," 3) "clear but also civil," and 4) "engaged, but not used."[21]

Adopting a Generous Orthodoxy

Christian liberals advance an informed understanding of scientific and ethical

---

17. Wallis 2008, 307.

18. Bass 2006, 42.

19. Wallis 2008, 14.

20. Bass 2006, 263.

21. Wallis 2008, 78.

issues among the Protestant perspective, while Christian conservatives advocate the doctrines of personal conversion and discipleship. However, this resulting split need not be. Brian McLaren seeks to embrace the contributions of both, being bolstered by their respective strengths and learning from their mistakes in order to move beyond the modern perspectives of liberal and conservative to a "post-liberal," "post-conservative," holistic understanding.[22]

Likewise defying labels of liberal and conservative,[23] emergents recognize the "irresolvable problems" with the left and the right, both politically and theologically. Rather than divisively choosing sides, they adopt the practice of "generous orthodoxy" – a phrase coined by Yale theologian Hans Frei[24] and the title of a subsequent work by Brian McLaren.[25] This generosity appreciates what *all* Christian movements have to offer, regardless of label or theological proclamation.[26]

In attempting to transcend this dichotomous standoff of liberal versus conservative, Frei advocates a middle ground between these polarized positions of modernity. With a generous orthodoxy, former liberals and conservatives can merge their once mutually exclusive theological approaches to a saner, more reasoned center. The result is an orthodoxy that is generous, both in understanding and in judgment. While a historical residue of each camp will remain, there will be a fresh willingness to address old questions in new ways, fostering "the pursuit of truth, the unity of the church, and the gracious character

---

22. McLaren 2004, 153, & 155.

23. Bass 2006, 306.

24. McLaren 2004, 10 and 14, in the second foreword written by John R. Franke; also http://en.wikipedia.org/wiki/Hans_Wilhelm_Frei.

25. McLaren 2004, cover.

26. Jones 2008, 7-8.

of the gospel."[27] Frei states that being generous while lacking the requisite framework of orthodoxy is worth nothing; even more foreboding is an orthodoxy that lacks generosity. Hence, there is the need for a generous orthodoxy.[28]

A Composite Understanding of Jesus

In his book *A Generous Orthodoxy*, McLaren seeks to move the modern world's theological dialog beyond the paralyzing impasse of liberal versus conservative into a "post-liberal," "post-conservative" inclusivity.[29] This, however, does not mean attempting to merely merge the two, but rather to *transcend* them, linking doctrine (orthodoxy) with practice (orthopraxy) – that is, binding spiritual theory to loving action from a biblical perspective.[30]

Towards this end, McLaren shares the various ways in which different manifestations of Christianity (that is, denominations) have shaped and influenced his appreciation for and understanding of Jesus.[31] This evokes a realization that God is a "unified, eternal, mysterious, relational community/family/society/entity of saving love."[32] Affirming his penchant of using hyperbole to provoke critical thinking among readers,[33] McLaren then asks the provocative, confrontational, tongue-in-cheek question, "Would Jesus be a

---

27. McLaren 2004, 14-16, in the second foreword written by John R. Franke.

28. Ibid., 18, in the second foreword written by John R. Franke.

29. McLaren 2004, 14-15, in the second foreword written by John R. Franke; McLaren 2004, 155.

30. McLaren 2004, 28.

31. Ibid., 49-71.

32. Ibid., 44.

33. Ibid., 27, 39.

Christian?"[34] After all, Jesus came to earth as a Jew.[35]

This sets the framework for the rest of McLaren's book, with each of its 16 chapters addressing one item in the book's cumbersomely long subtitle: *Why I am a missional, evangelical, post/protestant, liberal/conservative, mystical/poetic, biblical, charismatic/contemplative, fundamentalist/Calvinist, Anabaptist/Anglican, Methodist, catholic, green, incarnational, depressed-yet-hopeful, emergent, unfinished Christian.*[36] Parallels to the sentiment of this lengthy subtitle are seen in a teaching of Henri Nouwen as summarized by Diana Butler Bass, imploring followers of Jesus to live in "the wide stream of Christian traditions, from desert monasticism to Orthodox icons, from medieval mysticisms to Latin American liberation theology."[37]

In *A Generous Orthodoxy*, McLaren does not seek to promote an all-encompassing and carefully articulated orthodoxy – one to conclusively end all orthodoxies[38] – but instead he shares his thoughts on what it might include so that productive dialogue can be advanced in constructing an orthodoxy that is generous, accepting, inclusive, and loving.[39] From this "postcritical" perspective – which is not to imply "uncritical"[40] – there is the latitude and freedom to embrace the positive and the good that can be found in every facet of Christianity – both current and historical – integrating their diverse and disparate elements into a new approach that is greater than its parts; one that is generous and

---

34. Ibid., 87.

35. Tickle 2008, Words, 45.

36. McLaren 2004, 115-338 (chapters 5-20).

37. Bass 2009, History, 286

38. McLaren 2004, 29, 329, 333-338, & 347.

39. Ibid., 338.

40. Ibid., 22.

emergent.[41]

McLaren sees "the real Jesus" as a composite of how He is portrayed and promoted by the various sects of Christianity.[42] This includes conservative Protestants (evangelicals) who see Jesus as dying to save them; pentecostals who see Jesus as a miraculous healer and giver of the Holy Spirit to guide them; Roman Catholics who see Jesus' resurrection as defeating death and liberating humanity; Eastern Orthodox Christians who see the incarnation of Jesus as bringing healing to creation; liberal protestants who see the example and teaching of Jesus as the impetus for social justice and compassion ministries; Anabaptists who seek a learning community of disciples as modeled by Jesus and His twelve; and lastly from the nonviolent liberation theology camp (common in Latin America, but not exclusively so[43]), a Jesus who leads them to activism, confronting injustice[44] and promoting peace.[45] Regarding this final facet, Wallis unequivocally states that "God hates injustice" and those who follow Him should as well.[46]

These seemingly distinct views become less alarming when considering that the Bible uses the word "save" as meaning both "rescue" and "heal."[47] With that understanding, a comforting commonality begins to materialize among the seemingly divergent understandings of Jesus.

"Why not celebrate them all?" McLaren quips. He is not alone, with people increasingly embracing new labels such as "post-protestant,

---

41. Ibid., 29.

42. Ibid., 74.

43. Ibid., 70.

44. Wallis 2008, 59.

45. McLaren 2004, 51-71 and summarized on 72-73.

46. Wallis 2008, 59.

47. McLaren 2004, 101.

post-denominational, post-liberal, and post-conservative."[48] Diana Butler Bass adds to this list the phrases "post-traditional" and "post-everything."[49] These all point to a new era, moving "beyond polarization and sectarianism" that has all too often been emblematic of Christendom throughout much of its history. Instead, they see a fuller, more comprehensive amalgamation of Jesus, embracing His many facets that have been separately identified and celebrated by His disparate factions of followers.[50] In this regard, McLaren wonders if a "*convergence* of postmodern Christians" from these assorted faith tenets can result in a "new life and hope."[51]

Not a Superior Theology

Will this transcendent understanding McLaren proposes produce a superior theology, the preeminent faith to forever end all theological dissensions and faith conflicts? McLaren unequivocally says no. Just as a person progressing from one life stage to the next does not result in growing towards a perfection of humanity, but rather merely experiences different manifestations of life, so too is it with theological formations. In this regard, McLaren avers that a generous orthodoxy is in reality merely an emerging one; it will never be complete or final until the very end, when the followers of Jesus enjoy their final homecoming to God.[52]

Being generous with orthodoxy, as McLaren advocates, is to not claim (or believe) to have all the answers to faith issues neatly organized and fully detailed, but rather to be lovingly seeking truth in a missional faith community; it is not a compilation of correct canons, but a lifelong endeavor, pursuing a deeper and

---

48. Ibid., 74.

49. Bass 2004, 20.

50. McLaren 2004, 74.

51. Ibid., 133; emphasis added to highlight the title and theme of this work.

52. Ibid., 323.

expanded understanding of who God is and being in relationship with Him.[53] This view is in sharp contrast to the advocacy of a systematic theology that will either implicitly or explicitly end all theological debates, being a perfect and final treatise on the subject. Such an assertion, in consideration of a "generous orthodoxy," is in actuality a great error.[54]

John R. Franke recalls the sage assertion that "reformed theology is reforming theology." It arose from the "concern for the ongoing reformation of the faith and practice of the church according to the Word of God in the context of ever-changing circumstances and situations" and in "the context of an ever-changing world characterized by a variety of cultural settings."[55] This concept of ongoing reformation is integral to McLaren's advocacy for a generous orthodoxy and is consistent with an emerging faith. Towards this end, he maintains that "we must be *always reforming*."[56]

It is therefore not surprising that Tony Jones declares that the emergent conversation is a dynamic dialogue as opposed to a static belief.[57] Tickle adds that the logic of the past 500 years is now being circumvented by narrative, which "speaks to the heart" and is then able to "direct and inform the mind."[58]

"We are committed to a generous orthodoxy in faith and practice – affirming the historic Christian faith and the biblical injunction to love one another even

---

53. Ibid., 333-335.

54. Ibid., 325 and 336, where McLaren cites Vincent Donovan.

55. John R. Franke, "Reforming Theology," http://www.nextreformation.com/wp-admin/resources/Reforming_Theology.pdf (accessed December 7, 2009). It first appeared in The Westminster Theological Journal 65:1 (Spring, 2003): 1-26.

56. McLaren 2004, 213-214.

57. Jones 2008, 235.

58. Tickle 2008, Emergence, 160.

when we disagree," says Tony Jones. "We embrace many historical spiritual practices, including prayer, meditation, contemplation, study, solitude, silence, service, and fellowship, believing that healthy theology cannot be separated from healthy spirituality."[59]

A "generous orthodoxy," concludes McLaren, "presumes that the [church's] divisions, though tragic, are superficial compared to Christianity's deep, though often unappreciated unity."[60] Regarding the great response to McLaren's book on this subject, Diana Butler Bass asserts, "The longing for an open, nonjudgmental form of Christian practice is a more widespread cultural phenomenon than most scholars of American religion have guessed."[61]

The Role of the Bible and the Influence of Jesus

What McLaren and others refer to as generous orthodoxy, Bass labels as "theological generosity," a liberality in understanding.[62] Tickle is even more direct in this discussion of theological generosity. She notes that those who read their Bible literally condemn those who do not as being liberal, questioning their very salvation. Conversely, those who see their Bible as being metaphorical and evolving condemn those who do not as being dangerous Christians with anemic faith. Neither side has an inviting or compelling perspective.[63]

In their stead, Tickle offers a third alternative, which she labels as "actualness," in which one's heart and mind "assimilate in concord with one another, never separately," realizing that the Bible is neither literal nor metaphorical, but is in

---

59. Jones 2008, 223.

60. McLaren 2004, 250.

61. Bass 2006, 319.

62. Ibid., 191.

63. Tickle 2008, Words, 37.

reality "the ineluctable cohesion of it." She was brought to her articulation of this realization slowly and gently as she studied and contemplated the words of Jesus.[64] In this regard, many emergents have set aside the divisive need to be certain in their theological musings, seeking wisdom in its stead.[65]

In supporting fashion, Tony Jones teaches that emergents hold four common commitments: 1) to God in the way of Jesus; 2) to the church in all its forms; 3) to God's world; and 4) to one another.[66] Regarding the first commitment to find God through Jesus, if there is common ground in Jesus, then emergents ask for and expect little else. This provides emergents with an overall acceptance of *all* Christian movements.

The second commitment of the church in all its forms – which is also elucidated in emergent Dispatch 1[67] – is likewise unifying. It is the emergents' embrace of all forms of the church, be it "Orthodox, Roman Catholic, Protestant, Pentecostal, [or] Anabaptist."[68] Additionally, emergents embrace the various manifestations of this diverse list, effectively encompassing the full gambit of Christian expression, from the formal to informal, form to function, orthodox to non-orthodox, traditional to contemporary, liturgical to liberated, ritualistic to creative, sacred to creative, deliberate to free-flowing, modern to postmodern, institutional to organic, and even pipe organ to electric guitar, as well as every flavor in between.[69]

Not surprisingly, the inherently imperative impulse of emergence is to be

---

64. Ibid., 38.

65. Bass 2006, 51.

66. Jones 2008, 222-225.

67. Ibid., 8.

68. Ibid., 223.

69. McLaren, 2004; this diverse list is derived from the book's subtitle and the explanation thereof.

"irenic and inclusive," not "elitist and critical."[70] This is not a new idea, however. Two millennia ago, Jesus found Himself confronted with exclusivity, and He countered it with inclusivity. As such, today's postmodern proclivity for pluralism and inclusiveness is embraced and modeled by emergents as a worthy emulation of the life of Jesus. Both Jesus and the emergents who follow Him welcome and embrace those who are different.[71] This is not so with the exclusive nature of the modern church, most of which require participants to "join their spiritual side" (such as following a list of dos and don'ts, being baptized, or "getting saved" in a presubscribed manner) before they are accepted, much less allowed to become a member.[72]

Just as the once disparate countries in Europe now enjoy a degree of unification in the European Union, in the form of a common currency and ease of travel across borders, Christians in America are now moving freely from church to church and even denomination to denomination. Increasingly, denominational allegiances are being disregarded as "an outmoded form of organized Christianity," the bureaucracies of which have suffocated the gospel out of many churches.[73] In their place, emergents seek to reclaim and emulate Jesus' interaction with society as a revolutionary.[74]

Shunning Consumerism

One area of opposition is to Christian is consumerism. Many Christians are becoming increasingly disappointed with the consumeristic methods of the congregational model of church and an institutionalized, "Walmart approach

---

70. Jones 2008, 224.

71. Gibbs 2005, 119 & 122.

72. Bass 2006, 35.

73. Jones 2008, 8-9.

74. Ibid., 21.

to spirituality."[75] "The church as we know it," asserts Wolfgang Simson, "is preventing the church as God wants it."[76] James Rutz states sententiously, albeit shockingly, that "Jesus wants his church back."[77] Paul Vieira, in his book *Jesus Has Left the Building,* adds, "The church Jesus started is the one He's going to finish with."[78] He presents seven chapters detailing what the church of Jesus looked like as the early church and presently manifests in the emergent church. Briefly, the early church of Jesus: 1) was "amphibious" (existing in two environments); 2) was "chaotic"; 3) "knew their teachers"; 4) was "ruined for the world"; 5) received their mission through prayer; 6) "remembered the poor"; and 7) "had a voice to the culture."[79]

Indeed, Jesus cannot be domesticated by "layers of bureaucracy, institutionalism, and dogma," or smothered by mass quantities of the "Jesus junk" that a consumerism mentality demands from the modern church, says Jones. "The gospel can't be packaged."[80]

Emergent Christianity is the response to this,[81] valuing the quality of worship over the quality of the church's "goods and services."[82] Reflecting this goods and services mentality, church growth experts tend to elevate music in the church to the level of entertainment – it is "the tail that wags the dog" – with the musicians

---

75. Lisa Miller, "House of Worship," Newsweek, January 11, 2010, under http://www.newsweek.com/id/228722 (accessed January 14, 2010), 2.

76. Simson 2009, xiii.

77. Rutz 2008, 156.

78. Vieira 2006, 124.

79. Ibid., 125-246.

80. Jones 2008, 36-37.

81. Ibid., 36-37.

82. Kimball 2003, 115.

performing and the congregation passively watching; that is, consuming what is being offered.[83] This seeker-sensitive mindset mistakenly equates loud music with better worship – the louder the better. Emergents, however, often embrace stillness and contemplation as a preferable form of worship and the means to enter into the presence of God[84] – "listening to God in silence."[85]

The hope is that the emerging church can free itself from the grasp of the Christian consumerism mentality, providing an experiential, participatory worship gathering to replace the consumer-oriented, spectator mindset that is prevalent in many modern churches today.[86] Viola and Barna trace the practice of church "seating for passive and docile crowds to watch a performance" back to the fourth century, when Constantine began constructing Christianity's first church buildings.[87]

Confirming this reality, Rutz notes that "pew warmers are passé. They are stuck at half past yesterday and simply not ready" for all that God has in store for them.[88] Conversely, in her interviews with mainline emergents, Bass encountered participants who describe worship using terms such as feeling, experience, and even mystery,[89] changing the church and its people in the process.[90] They do not concern themselves with the polarized debate over contemporary versus traditional, instead incorporating music from vastly varying

---

83. Bass 2006, 204.

84. Ibid., 118-119.

85. Ibid., 126.

86. Kimball 2003, 112.

87. Viola and Barna 2008, 22.

88. Rutz 2005, 87.

89. Bass 2006, 177.

90. Ibid., 180.

and disparate origins.[91]

A Postmodern Practice

In their book *Emerging Churches*, authors Eddie Gibbs and Ryan Bolger define emerging churches as "communities that practice the way of Jesus within postmodern cultures." Expanding on this definition, they proceed to advance nine characteristics or practices of the emergent church: 1) identification with Jesus; 2) transformation of secular space; 3) life in community; 4) hospitality towards strangers; 5) serving generously; 6) being producers; 7) creativity; 8) leading as a body; and 9) merging ancient and contemporary spirituality. The bulk of their book elucidates these nine elements.[92]

Scot McKnight, Anabaptist theologian and professor of religious studies at North Park University, advances a more focused definition of emerging churches, stating, "Emerging churches are missional communities emerging in postmodern culture and consisting of followers of Jesus seeking to be faithful to the orthodox Christian faith in their place and time."[93] Embedded in this idea of being missional is the recognition of not being "end users of the gospel" for personal benefit alone, but instead being equipped and sent into the world to love and serve others.[94]

Avoiding a formal definition, Paul Vieira takes a stab at describing this move in his aptly titled book *Jesus Has Left the Building*. He says that as people emerge from the traditional church, most leave the building of the church, even to the point of appearing religiously disinterested and bored. Shunning traditional leadership roles and authoritative positions, they stealthily resurface, meeting

---

91. Ibid., 182.

92. Gibbs 2005, 44-45.

93. http://blog.beliefnet.com/jesuscreed/2006/11/bloglossary.html, accessed October 20, 2010.

94. Pagitt 2003, 146.

informally in "cafés, lounges, homes and apartments, restaurants, or anywhere a few friends can come together to connect in casual dialogue." They are in hiding, metaphorically in Egypt – just as God hid both Joseph and Jesus in Egypt, protecting them from harm and attack, while awaiting God's timing and purpose. From there, they will be called to "change the face of Christianity."[95]

The Emergent Mindset

In 2006, Tony Jones visited eight emergent churches in the United States. There he conducted one-on-one interviews and facilitated focus groups with participants so that he could better understand their collective mindset about what they valued in the emergent movement. In doing so, three reoccurring trends became apparent. Jones presented this list with a bit of trepidation, ironically noting that emergents eschew lists. He also gave the humble acknowledgment that his list may be incomplete.[96]

First, these emergents felt a profound disappointment with the modern church. However, even though they had largely lost faith in the institutional church, their faith in Jesus had remained intact and strong.[97] Confirming this, Gibbs notes that emergents are burdened with a growing conviction that serious problems exist in the modern church, and that it is in dire need of a fresh evaluation and reformulation in light of a solidly gospel – that is, biblical – perspective.[98] Vieira pointedly states that emergents do not feel safe in the church institution.[99]

---

95. Vieira 2006, 75-76.

96. Jones 2008, 70-72.

97. Ibid., 70 & 172.

98. Gibbs 2005, 48.

99. Vieira 2006, 76.

Diana Butler Bass notes, "Jesus fascinates millions, but Christianity, the religion that began with Jesus, leaves countless people cold."[100] Dan Kimball concurs, devoting an entire book to the subject – appropriately titled *They Like Jesus but Not the Church*. His interviews with unchurched postmoderns revealed their widespread dislike and mistrust of the institutional church, along with a simultaneous respect for Jesus and an openness to talk about Him.[101] Interestingly, what they don't like is essentially the biblically unsupportable manifestations of the modern church.[102] It is largely the attitudes and rhetoric of today's church that produces negative perceptions among the unchurched, creating a chasm that blocks them from listening to and trusting in its gospel.[103] However, this concerns Henri Nouwen. "When we say 'I love Jesus, but I hate the church,' we end up losing not only the church but Jesus too. The challenge is to forgive the church," but "the church seldom asks us for forgiveness."[104]

Second, emergents have a desire for the inclusion of people with diverse views and spiritual perspectives. This is not to imply an anything goes, indecisive theology,[105] but rather it is the result of a strong comprehension that they might very well be wrong in the beliefs which they espouse.[106] This requires a discerning spirit[107] and a humble heart. Specifically, Jones uses the phrase "humble

---

100. Bass 2009, 1.

101. Kimball 2007, 11-12.

102. Ibid., 68.

103. Ibid., 236.

104. Henri Nouwen, Bread for the Journey (New York: HarperCollins, 1997), 318.

105. Jones 2008, 90.

106. Ibid., 71.

107. Bass 2006, 92-93.

hermeneutics," or more philosophically, "epistemic humility."[108] McLaren, in advancing his call for a generous orthodoxy, says that it "doesn't take itself too seriously...it is humble."[109] In like manner, Bass refers to the "humility of spiritual liberality."[110] Tickle concurs, eloquently opining, "We have become lost in a wilderness of scholarship that forgot to bring faith and humility along for the trek."[111]

According to Randy, a member of an emerging mainline church who Bass interviewed, emergents have the "ability to hold creative tensions," not only with diverse musical styles and genres, but also along the continuum of theological doctrine.[112] Regarding this oft-polarizing issue of theology, the key question becomes "Are we going to stand together in unity despite our theological differences, or will we allow them to divide us?"[113] The goal is an actual, tangible embrace of divergent theological perspectives without any indication of division, dissention, or discord.[114] However, this practice of diversity is not to be mistaken for secular relativism, but rather is "the active construction of a boundary-crossing community."[115]

Just as theological diversity is cherished in the emergent church, so too is diversity in politics, culture, and race. Lest this be dismissed as inappropriate or

---

108. Jones 2008, 141.

109. McLaren 2004, 171.

110. Bass 2006, 193.

111. Tickle 2008 Words, 9.

112. Bass 2006, 145.

113. Dale 2009, 167.

114. Ibid., 167.

115. Bass 2006, 148; consider Mark 10:21; John 11:3; John 11:5; John 13:1; John 13:23; John 15:9; John 15:12; John 20:2.

unbiblical, consider Jesus' profound love for all people,[116] as well as the culturally diverse gatherings of His initial followers, in which Jews, Gentiles, Samaritans, and Africans all coexisted in community for mutual service and integrated worship.[117] As such, says Bass, the emergent church is demographically an "untidy place."[118]

Philip Yancey agrees, noting that diversity complicates things rather than simplifies them. The church offers – or should offer – the potential for people of different ages, economic classes, backgrounds, and opinions to interact with each other and pursue a common faith. Homogeny, although a comfortable human tendency, was not demonstrated by the early church, where divisions based on gender, race, and social standing were nonexistent.[119]

Mark Galli states that there is an increased awareness and appreciation for the array of races, nationalities, and ethnicities in the world. He notes that when the church of Jesus embraces an increase in diversity, Christianity has been shown to flourish.[120] This push for diversity, however, is not a "capitulation to political liberalism," notes Bass, but more correctly "a deeply biblical and profoundly theological practice."[121]

Josh Loveless pointedly highlights this imperative need for a diversity of perspectives, stating that seeking relationships with people just like oneself is simply a form of self-worship. "Imagine," he continues, "what [it] might look

---

116. Ibid., 148-149; again, consider Mark 10:21, John 11:3, John 11:5, John 13:1, John 13:23, John 15:9, John 15:12, John 20:2.

117. Ibid., 149.

118. Ibid., 256.

119. Yancey 2008, 119.

120. Mark Galli, "In the Beginning, Grace," Christianity Today (October 2009): 27.

121. Bass 2006, 150.

like if members of each generation were invited to a seat at the table – to teach one another about theology and ecclesiology." He cites Earl Creps's book, *Reverse Mentoring: How Young Leaders Can Transform the Church and Why We Should Let Them*, which explains how interactions between the young and the old can be mutually beneficial.[122]

This push for diversity is not solely the imperative of emergent Christians, however. In 1848, Horace Bushnell advocated that religious diversity is the pathway towards "a more complete and perfect whole."[123] In striving to comprehend diverse sects and theologies, he saw a universal truth emerging as harmony.[124] For it is in "embracing and comprehending all," wrote Bushnell, that "Christian souls will ring in peals of harmony, as a chime that is voiced by the truth."[125]

This flows into Jones's third common characteristic of emergence as a "hope-filled orientation," more technically referred to as an "eschatological hope."[126] McLaren expertly exemplifies this emergent trait, admitting that he has "an uncorrected leaning toward optimism and hope."[127] This is concurred with and supported by emergent Dispatch 15, which says that "emergents hold to a hope-filled eschatology."[128]

Emergent Theology

---

122. Loveless 2009, 62.

123. Bushnell 2010, 387.

124. Bushnell 2010, 459; Bass 2009 History, 243.

125. Bushnell 2010, 459.

126. Jones 2008, 72.

127. McLaren 2004, 25.

128. Jones 2008, 177.

Springing from the aforementioned desire for inclusion is Tony Jones's seventh emergent dispatch, which affirms that emergents seek "an envelope of friendship and reconciliation that must surround all debates about doctrine and dogma."[129] They see the need that many people have to be able to accept or reject outright specific doctrinal stances and theological determinations as "an articulation of modern Christianity" and the result of human intellect, which too often fails its followers.[130] Indeed, to be completely certain on a specific theological stance suggests that all other perspectives and opinions are inherently in error. This leads to an unwavering imposition of one's beliefs upon others.[131] Conversely, emergents desire to be wise about God more so than being certain about their theology.[132]

While many modern Christians aver that (or act as if) the Bible is simple and easy to understand, emergents see the Bible as increasingly more complex with each successive read. They do not view questioning the Bible and their faith as defiance, but instead as an act of integrity.[133] If nothing else, the emergent church is, by intention, a safe place to ask challenging and difficult questions.[134] Emergents also see the danger in placing themselves in theological silos, which is one reason why they embrace diversity within their community. Diversity effectively serves to lessen the risk of grave theological error or heresy occurring.[135]

---

129. Ibid., 78.

130. Ibid., 78-79.

131. Ibid., 141.

132. Bass 2006, 51.

133. Jones 2008, 110.

134. Gibbs 2005, 46.

135. Jones 2008, 113.

In this regard, Bass notes the tendency of emergents to study the Bible with seriousness, while avoiding literal interpretations. They intend to avoid following in the dogmatic footsteps of conservative evangelicals who read most things in the Bible with a literal eye and seek proof-texts in order to make unequivocal pronouncements over esoteric moral and ethical issues.[136] This narrow approach of theological rigidity leaves emergents feeling "intellectually constrained." In light of this, Bass asserts that a large portion of the North America Christian community has grown to exhibit a "strangely circumscribed intellectual character," which she labels as an "anti-intellectual intellectualism."[137] In its place, emergent pilgrims contend for an open intellectualism as an imperative characteristic of true spirituality.[138] Asking questions in the emergent church is not only accepted, but also encouraged. This is a compelling draw to the increasing number of people who desire a more holistic and inclusive "open Christianity."[139]

Emergents, many of whom grew up experiencing the seeker-sensitive mindset regarding church, have cast aside the pursuit of easy theological answers. Instead, their movement is a reaction to that, one that seeks to reclaim the tradition of deep theological struggles that are rightly a part of pursuing faith in Jesus.[140] In fact, the seeker-sensitive style of the modern church and the consumerism mentality behind it is largely shunned by emerging generations. Kimball recalls visiting a large church, where he experienced what he describes as the quintessential seeker-sensitive service, observing that there was virtually no one under the age

---

136. Bass 2006, 188.

137. Ibid., 189.

138. Ibid., 191.

139. Ibid., 198.

140. Jones 2008, 109.

of thirty, because emergents are seeking exactly the opposite.[141]

Emergents recognize that the typical hour-long Sunday service is resource-intensive and, at the same time, fails to disciple people and change lives.[142] Many are beginning to realize that the true message of Jesus is countercultural. Their response is to reject the consumer mindset and ethical perspective of the suburbanite seeker who expects comfort, options, and one-stop spiritual shopping. Narcissism is giving way to sacrificial serving and missional actions.[143] As pastor and author Rick Warren unequivocally warns in the opening line of his mega-selling book *The Purpose Driven Life*, "It's not about you." Creation was made for His purpose; "it all starts with God."[144]

Emergents painfully realize that this consumeristic approach to spirituality all too often results in Christians who effectively make Jesus into their own image of who they want or need Him to be. In the process, they lose sight of who Jesus is and what He has done.[145] Jesus did not come into the world and die for mankind so that His followers could live comfortable and complacent lives, but rather so that they could pick up their crosses, follow Him, and die to themselves.[146] Although the seeker-sensitive movement of the latter part of the twentieth century did much to remove superfluous tradition from religious practices, it also treated attendees as consumers rather than adherents, producing the unexpected side effect of relegating the church to the status of an "optional

---

141. Kimball 2003, 101-102.

142. Simson 2009, xix.

143. Wallis 2008, 34.

144. Rick Warren, The Purpose Driven Life (Grand Rapids, MI: Zondervan, 2002), 17.

145. McLaren 2004, 110.

146. Barna 2005, 41.

consumer product."[147]

Vintage Faith

Given this perspective, emergents opt for a spiritual pursuit that Kimball calls "vintage faith." He describes it as an organic approach to a worship gathering, one that is experiential in nature, focusing on fluidity and freedom, as practiced by the church throughout the ages. It jettisons the orderly, systematic, logical, and progressive style that the modern church practices; it is not a passive, consumer-oriented service. Instead, vintage faith is community-oriented, participatory, multisensory, and Spirit-led; it allows a transcendent God to be encountered.[148] Participants come to church not to be fed but to learn to feed themselves.[149] Bass cites that many of the emergents she encountered talk freely and easily about the work of the mysterious third part of the Trinity, the Holy Spirit, as being integral in their spiritual pilgrimage.[150]

This role of the Holy Spirit in the vintage faith expression touches the yearnings of emergents, as they inherently place more trust in the movement and direction of God's Spirit than they do in the methodology of the modern way of doing church. In short, the Holy Spirit's agenda trumps the plans of leaders and the traditions of the church.[151] It is not surprising, then, that emergents resist services, systems, and schema that attempt to put an orderly box and neat bow around God, obscuring the mystery and holistic nature of God and spirituality

---

147. Matthew Green, "The Church Dropout," Charisma (December 2009): 30.

148. Kimball 2003, 121-130.

149. Ibid., 223.

150. Bass 2006, 242.

151. Jones 2008, 61; Gibbs 2005, 127.

in the process.[152]

McLaren talks about a "God-given thirst" that is exemplified by today's vintage faith emergents; it prods them to move beyond the status quo of where they are, transcending into newer and fresher spiritual plains. This is not just happening now but has in fact happened at numerous times throughout church history. At each iteration it is messy and imperfect, but it is progress.[153] In recognition of this, emergents have an innate desire to learn from all of church history.[154] Additionally, the experiential element of vintage faith is one that resonates with today's postmodern culture, where members learn experientially and then later validate that experience through knowledge.[155]

The Revolution

In his watershed book *Revolution*, George Barna looks at how cultural change is intersecting with spiritual transformation to produce "an explosion of spiritual energy and activity...an unprecedented reengineering of America's faith" that will change the "religious landscape." He calls it "the revolution,"[156] and says that it has the potential to be a significant faith recalibration,[157] serving to "advance the Church" and "redefine the church." (Barna uses the lowercased "church" to refer to the typical "congregational-based faith experience," while the capitalized

---

152. Kimball 2003, 217.

153. McLaren 2004, 322-323.

154. Jones 2008, 230, citing
http://www.theooze.com/articles/article.cfm?id=1151&page=1, accessed October 20, 2010.

155. Kimball 2003, 186.

156. Barna 2005, viii.

157. Ibid., ix.

"Church" is all true believers and followers of Jesus, regardless of their setting or context.)[158]

Without directly using the labels of emergent and emerging, Barna nonetheless proceeds to define this revolution using many of the same expressions and persuasive imperatives that emanate from the emergent conversation. However, he does directly connect the revolution with postmodernity. Citing seven trends (see Appendix B for a list of all seven) that are ushering in this spiritual revolution, the second is "the rise of a new view of life," courtesy of the pervasive postmodern mindset permeating the world today.[159] While it can be said that this revolution coexists with or runs parallel to emergence, it is perhaps more likely that the revolution transcends emergence or emanates from it. (This idea of transcending emergence will be addressed in great detail later on in this chapter in the section labeled "The Great Emergence.")

Calling the present era the revolutionary age, Barna says it is a quiet revolution of which few are aware, including the media, academia, society, and the church.[160] In defining the word "revolution" generically, he uses words such as "overthrow," "radical," and "pervasive." This burgeoning faith movement, which he also calls "revolution," will purportedly produce a "lasting change"; it is a result of millions of Jesus' followers "repudiating tepid systems and practices of the Christian faith and introducing a wholesale shift in how faith is understood, integrated, and influencing the world."[161]

Despite an unprecedented busyness in the world today, these faith revolutionaries are returning to a first-century lifestyle and value system, intentionally embracing it as the only tenable solution to a world that is out

---

158. Ibid., x.

159. Ibid., 42-43.

160. Ibid., 9.

161. Ibid., 11.

of control.[162] Barna cites seven passions of these revolutionaries, which are consistent with life in the early church. These passions are: 1) intimate worship; 2) faith-based conversations; 3) intentional spiritual growth; 4) servanthood; 5) resource investment; 6) spiritual friendships; and 7) family faith – noting that two thousand years ago the home was essentially the church. (These are not to be confused with the seven trends that are ushering in the revolution. Both the seven trends and the seven passions are listed in Appendix B.)[163]

For those who seize these passions fully and intentionally integrate them into their lives, a spiritual transformation takes place. Perhaps shockingly, the primary manifestations of these transformations are found in ministries operating outside of the local church. These are not necessarily parachurch movements either, but rather "mini-movements" such as homeschooling, "simple church fellowships," "biblical worldview groups," "marketplace ministries," "spiritual disciplines networks," and "Christian creative arts guilds."[164] For the revolutionary, the modern local church is not the epicenter of their transformation.[165]

Barna's research, published in 2005, shows that this group of revolutionaries numbers twenty million strong. They dismiss churches that play religious games and offer programs that produce no spiritual fruit, refusing to support religious institutionalism in the process. Instead, the members of the revolution have great zeal for intimacy with God and look to the Bible for guidance. In the process, they are reshaping society and the church, ushering in a legacy of spiritual reformation.[166]

As with any revolution, there is resistance from established institutions

---

162. Ibid., 12-17.

163. Ibid., 22-24.

164. Ibid., 52-55.

165. Ibid., 58.

166. Ibid., 12-17.

clinging to the status quo and resisting change. This has happened with every significant move in the church that Jesus launched; the same is currently happening and will continue to happen with this revolution.[167]

The Red Pill

It may only be coincidental – or perhaps a confirmation of emergence's cultural connection, significance, and relevance – that the 1999 release of the movie *The Matrix* corresponds with the beginnings of emergence. It is perhaps intentional that Neo, the hero of the movie, is also the nickname given to the sage protagonist in Brian McLaren's 2001 classic emergent tome, *A New Kind of Christian*.[168]

In a pivotal point in the movie's early stages, the character of Morpheus says to his protégée Neo, "This is your last chance. After this, there is no turning back. You take the blue pill – the story ends, you wake up in your bed and believe whatever you want to believe. You take the red pill – you stay in Wonderland and I show you how deep the rabbit-hole goes."[169] This poignant scene becomes a coded metaphor for those misfits from the established church culture who have begun a move towards emergence: "Did you take the red pill?"[170]

Karen Ward, vicar and abbess at the Church of the Apostles in Seattle, Washington, declares: "The emerging church is being willing to take the red pill, going down the rabbit hole, and enjoying the ride. It is Dorothy not in Kansas anymore, yet finding her way home. It is Superman braving kryptonite to

---

167. Ibid., 111-112.

168. McLaren, 2001, 4.

169. The Internet Movie Database, http://www.imdb.com/title/tt0133093/quotes (accessed November 23, 2009).

170. Jones 2008, 58.

embrace Krypton. It is sight seeking wider vision, relationships seeking expanded embrace, and spirituality seeking holistic practice. It is," she concludes, "a 'road of destination' where Christ followers, formerly of divergent pasts, are meeting up in the missional present and moving towards God's future."[171]

Divergent pasts, meeting up and moving towards the future: emergence is indeed a movement towards unity.

---

171. Gibbs 2005, 27, quoting Karen Ward.

More Than Emergent

Labeling himself as an emergent, Tony Jones proclaims that emergence is just one "manifestation of the coming dramatic shift in what it means to be Christian."[1] Paradoxically, emergents are both "pioneers" and "expatriates," while their church "is a mash-up of old and new, of theory and practice, of men and women, and of mainline, evangelical, and increasingly Roman Catholic Christians,"[2] with approximately one-fourth of emergents having a Roman Catholic background and formation.[3] These emergents are attempting to reconcile the unbiblical distinctions between the clergy and the laity; they are reclaiming the concept of the "priesthood of believers."[4]

The result is an intriguing nexus of the theoretical (that is, theology or orthodoxy; literally "straight thinking or right opinion"[5]) and the practical (that is, praxis or orthopraxis; literally, "right practice").[6] Towards this goal, emerging Christians have given up the hopeless and polarizing pursuit of "pure doctrine" – that is, embracing a list of philosophical distinctions – opting instead for the more

---

1. Jones 2008, xviii.

2. Ibid., xviii-xix.

3. Tickle 2008, Emergence, 104.

4. Viola and Barna 2008, 105-143 (specifically 122 and 141); 1 Peter 2:5, 9

5. McLaren 2004, 23.

6. Jones 2008, xix.

practical pursuit of right actions and examined practices.[7] Almost two thousand years ago, Paul recognized this human tendency toward dogmatic doctrinal debates when he warned Timothy about those who have "an unhealthy interest in controversies and quarrels about words," the pursuit of which produces "envy, strife, malicious talk, evil suspicions and constant friction"; these people "have been robbed of the truth and...think that godliness is a means to financial gain" (1 Timothy 6:4).

In elucidating the emerging church, Phyllis Tickle evokes the day's computer vernacular, calling it a network that is "ongoing, open-source, and self-organizing." She further declares that this system is not without error and will never be complete; it is "alive, flexible, changing, growing, diverse, and egalitarian."[8] If this description conjures up the Internet, then consider that with no formal leadership, no corporate control, and no center of operations, the Internet proves that decentralized structure is not an oxymoron.[9]

In a similar manner, the emergent church does not function like the ecclesiastical movements of the past, but instead operates "more like an open source network and less like a hierarchy or bureaucracy."[10] In fact, Rick Warren asserts that *network* will replace *hierarchy*.[11] Emergents adamantly assert that a proportionately inverse relationship exists between bureaucracy and true, biblical Christianity. While not all bureaucratic governances are bad (the Department of Motor Vehicles is a worthy and necessary bureaucracy) and not all hierarchies lead to bureaucracy, there is nonetheless a normal human inclination for formal organizational structures to become self-preserving bureaucracies that

---

7. Bass 2006, 74-75.

8. Tickle, 2008 Words, 10.

9. Jones 2008, 180-181. See Appendix A, "Dispatch 16."

10. Ibid., 180. See Appendix A, "Dispatch 16."

11. Morgan 2008, 44.

increasingly lose sight of their original purpose and cause.[12]

One of the very reasons that emergent churches are hard to define is that they consist of decentralized communities.[13] To exemplify this reality, Brandon O'Brien notes that even the Emergent Village, the once unofficial voice of the emergent movement, opted to decentralize its organization in late 2008 by eliminating its national coordinator position and becoming more egalitarian.[14] From this perspective, Simson also notes the need for a "flat" structure for emergent churches.[15] Their focus is on the organism of the church, not the organization of the church.[16] Many of these emerging churches, in their effort to emulate the biblical kingdom model, adamantly eschew top-down control and centralized oversight for their leadership structure, if they have any formal leaders at all. Indeed, some emergents are experimenting with leaderless groups.[17]

With both the Internet and the emergent church being equality-minded and inclusive, the concurrence of their birth and growth is neither surprising nor coincidental. Likewise, it is not surprising that both the Internet and emergence manifest decentralization and shared control. There are three interrelated Internet concepts that provide additional emergent clarity in this regard: a scale-free network, open-source software, and wikis.[18]

First, the reality of a scale-free network is that it operates somewhere between

---

12. Jones 2008, 180.

13. Simson 2009, 75.

14. Brandon O'Brien, "Emergent's Divergence," Christianity Today (January 2009): 13.

15. Simson 2009, 75.

16. Ibid., xix.

17. Gibbs 2005, 192.

18. Jones 2008, 181.

the polar extremes of hierarchical control (Simson notes that fear produces the desire for control[19]) and arbitrary randomness. It is essentially self-sustaining, able to powerfully propagate with great speed and dexterity. This characteristic also exemplifies the emergent church.[20]

Next, open-source software consists of freely disclosed code, resources, and tools, which users can share, adapt, and modify without restriction or oversight. It is truly egalitarian in nature, again embodying the essence of emergence.[21]

Lastly, a wiki is a collaborative website that exists as a user-controlled, user-regulated database of information.[22] A wiki (specifically Wikipedia) possesses six characteristics that parallel traits of the emergent church: open access, trust, mutual accountability, agility, connectivity, and messiness.[23]

Mainline Emergence and Beyond

While much of this discussion of emergence springs from a conservative perspective, Bass notes that emergence is not the exclusive domain of evangelicals.[24] To support this assertion, a Google search using the word "emergent" (or variants thereof) paired with virtually any Protestant denomination (such as Anglican, Baptist, Quaker), Christian subset (for example, Protestant, Roman Catholic, Greek Orthodox), or world faith (Hindu, Buddhist, Jewish, or Muslim) results in a plethora of matches. Some of the above-named faiths (along with many not listed) have established

---

19. Simson 2009, xix.

20. Jones 2008, 181.

21. Ibid., 181.

22. http://en.wikipedia.org/wiki/Wiki, accessed November 18, 2009.

23. Jones 2008, 182-190.

24. Bass 2006, 319.

groups focusing on emergent conversation for their particular tenet of
ideology (Anglimergent, Presbymergent, Baptimergent, MethoMergent Lab,
Luthermergent, and Synagogue 3000 are several that were quickly identified).

Just as postmodernism is a global evolution, the emergence that is birthed
from it is also a widespread phenomenon. Addressing this from a mainline
Protestant perspective is Diana Butler Bass in her book *Christianity for the Rest
of Us*. She opens by admitting that mainline (that is, liberal) Protestantism is
in trouble, with declining attendance and a loss of significance.[25] This is not a
hopeless situation, however, as there are signs of revitalization at *some* mainline
churches with energized growth and renewed relevance, focusing on tradition
(not traditionalism), practice (not purity), and wisdom (not certainty).[26] Citing
a label determined by Bible scholar Marcus Borg, Bass calls the emergence she sees
within mainline churches as "transformational Christianity."[27]

Looking at selected mainline congregations that exhibit this transformational
Christianity (that is, emergence), Bass shares ten signposts of renewal: hospitality,
discernment, healing, contemplation, testimony, diversity, justice, worship,
reflection, and beauty.[28] In doing so, these churches are on a path toward
transforming lives, transforming congregations, and transforming the world,[29]
hence engendering Bass's label of transformational Christianity.[30]

Furthermore, although the preceding discussion of emergence focuses on

---

25. Ibid., 6-7.

26. Ibid., 45-53.

27. Ibid., 264-265.

28. Ibid., 77-214. Each of the ten items in this list is covered in detail in part 2
of the book, chapters 5 through 14.

29. Ibid., 219-278. These three items are covered in detail in part 3 of the book,
chapters 15 through 17.

30. Ibid., 265.

the United States, the USA is not its exclusive domain. A parallel movement (or perhaps a preceding one) has been growing in the United Kingdom, albeit under a different moniker: alternative worship, or alt.worship. A prime tenet of alternative worship is the desire to reduce the exclusion of those who might be on the fringes of society and alienated by the traditional church.[31] This international aspect is confirmed in emergent Dispatch 5, which says "The emergent movement is not exclusively North America; it is growing around the globe."[32]

Initially, alternative worship arose as a "contextual reaction" to the rave subculture in the UK, which has sprouted new manifestations of church that are indigenous to the club subculture.[33] This is an outgrowth of and reaction to an extensive club scene in the UK, which is not as of yet as fully developed in the US. It is estimated that, in the UK, 60 percent of the eighteen to thirty-five demographic identify with the club culture, albeit to varying degrees. (The source of this estimate is Steve Cockram, at the time the leader of Ascension, "a high-profile outreach ministry within the club culture.")[34] This profound shift in the UK is preceding the US by about twenty years. As such, the UK manifestation of emergence is a predictor and precursor of what can be expected as emergence in North America continues to unfold.[35]

Tony Jones further cites emergent meetings in Latin America, Europe, Asia, Africa, Australia, and New Zealand.[36] Concerning these same geographies, Phyllis Tickle notes that these peoples' respective shift in Christian thinking

---

31. Jones 2008, 52 & 54.

32. Ibid., 52; see Appendix A, "Dispatch 5."

33. Gibbs 2005, 81.

34. Ibid., 25.

35. Tickle 2008, Emergence, 121.

36. Jones 2008, 54.

parallels those in the United States.[37] Gibbs and Bolger, making a bold, sweeping statement, assert that the universal church is, in fact, an emerging one. It is the body of Christ present and at work in this world; it is in the process of becoming; it exists as a pilgrim, living in a provisional present reality, moving towards a final consummation; and it engages a diverse array of cultures, injecting the influence of redemption in them.[38]

House Churches

A recurring emergent theme is that of community, be it a learning community, a relational community, a border-crossing community, a transforming community, a faith community, a missional community, or a missional faith community. Taken as a composite, these various community adjectives embrace the totality of the emergent community yearning. Indeed, today's faithful realize that faith is best practiced in community.[39] Recall that member participation, a standard in the early church, was a trait that was lost during the Constantinian Era.[40] It is within community that "real spiritual formation happens."[41]

The primary intent of these communities is to facilitate their participants' predilection for relationality, both personal and spiritual. In accomplishing this, Wolfgang Simson has identified five basic elements common to the early church and current-day house churches. They are eating together, teaching, sharing, praying and prophesying, and promoting mutual accountability.[42]

---

37. Tickle 2008, Emergence, 121.

38. Gibbs 2005, 43.

39. Bass 2009, History, 299.

40. Gibbs 2005, 170-171; Viola and Barna 2008, 25.

41. Pagitt 2003, 26.

42. Simson 2009, 33-42.

House churches (and the various expressions thereof – home church, simple church, and organic church[43]) are prime manifestations of this yearning for community, often existing in loosely connected networks.[44] These home gatherings have a family atmosphere, expect every member to participate, and have an inherent mistrust of authority and institutional hierarchy,[45] as is the case with the early church.[46] C. Peter Wagner notes that house churches simply follow the pattern in the New Testament of Christians meeting together in people's homes. They avoid the distinction between pastor and member, with all who are present participating as God leads them, mutually ministering to each other, and caring for one another.[47]

Wolfgang Simson asserts that he sees God reclaiming the home, with it once again becoming "the natural habitat of the church."[48] This declaration is bolstered by fact. Donald E. Miller, citing a recent survey by the Pew Forum on Religion and Public Life, indicates that 7 percent of Americans affirm that they "attend religious services in someone's home." This occurs in a manner quite contrary to mainstream conceptions of church.[49]

This movement of home-based churches is often associated with emergence, although not exclusively so. Miller notes that progressive Roman Catholics are also starting home churches.[50] In fact, during the Reformation Martin Luther

---

43. Miller 2010, 2.

44. Gibbs 2005, 110; Rutz 2005, 2.

45. Miller 2010, 2.

46. Miller 2010, 2; Simson 2009, 17.

47. Wagner 2004, 135.

48. Simson 2009, 51.

49. Miller 2010, 1.

50. Ibid., 2-3.

recognized the need to reinstitute the house church model of the early church, but he did not follow through in implementing it.[51]

Other comparable labels for house churches include "open church," "organic church," "simple church," and the aforementioned "vintage church." According to Tony Dale, Felicity Dale, and George Barna, "house churches," "simple churches," "organic churches," and "missional churches" are interchangeable names. However, they prefer the label "simple church," as it encompasses but is not limited to meeting in houses.[52] Alternately, others do make distinctions among these various labels. However, exploring these nuances exceeds the intent of this work and is not necessary to advance the discussion. The primary principle to be communicated is simply that emergents seek a different form of church from what is currently occurring, with house churches being one such option.[53]

Spirit-Led Meetings

"Organic church" is a term advanced for a particular type of house church. Frank Viola and George Barna assert that not all house churches are organic, nor do all organic churches meet in houses. However, the organic church principles they advocate serve to illustrate and advance the overall discussion. The organic church, they declare, is simply one "born out of spiritual life" and not a construct of human institution and religious programming. Instead, organic churches are "Spirit-led, open-participatory meetings and nonhierarchical leadership";[54] they are the polar opposite of the contemporary church's clergy-led, institutionally driven methodology.[55] Regardless of designation, the intent of the house church

---

51. Simson 2009, 24.

52. Dale 2009, xii, 9, & 15.

53. See Appendix E, "Sources of Ongoing Study."

54. Viola and Barna 2008, xix.

55. Viola and Barna 2008, xix; Tickle 2008, Emergence, 153.

initiative is to eliminate "the middlemen (the pastors, the committees, and the denomination)" and deal "directly with God…helping him to create a new world" in the process.[56]

This inclination of emergent peoples to form house churches and what Jones calls "new monastic communities"[57] epitomize a recapturing of their inherent desire for relationality.[58] In this regard, consider the Trinity as the preeminent exemplifier of community.[59] With mankind made in the image of the Creator (Genesis 1:26), the embodiment of spiritual characteristics in physical form, it is no wonder that the created have a natural inclination for the communal reality of the Creator.

A Desire for Personal Transformation

Emanating from this desire for greater relationality is an even greater proclivity for personal transformation. Wallis declares: "Personal transformation is necessary for social movements."[60] This is a path that can be greatly facilitated within the functioning fellowship of a true faith community. Emergents have grown weary of merely amassing biblical knowledge and being able to articulate a systematic theology for the sake of scholarship, as doing so does not produce personal transformation. This leads many to seek new methods of discipleship,

---

56. Rutz 2005, 28.

57. Though Jones evokes the phrase, he doesn't define it. This author understands him to mean an monastery-like assembly of Jesus-followers, perhaps even intent on pursuing an ascetic existence.

58. Jones 2008, 166.

59. Viola 2008, 128.

60. Wallis 2008, 13.

including small groups[61] (which epitomize the New Testament church,[62] often acting as "surrogate families"[63]), and empowering the laity –another characteristic of the early church.[64] Indeed, in his letter to the Romans, Paul affirms that the laity is "complete in knowledge and competent to instruct one another" (Romans 15:14). It is no wonder, then, that in the spirit of the Protestant Reformation's doctrine advocating the priesthood of believers, James Rutz boldly states: "The first thing we do, let's kill all the sermons."[65]

Greater Intimacy

Another key attraction of the home-based house church is that it encourages the smaller, more intimate gatherings toward which the emergent generation gravitates.[66] The expected results are that participants will grow their character, soothe their sorrows, and develop their spiritual gifts; they will have their wounds healed, their spirits lifted, their minds taught, and their souls discipled, while regularly experiencing a true encounter with God.[67]

Aside from a loss of denominational or ecclesiastical oversight and control, a common criticism of laity-led house churches is the perceived threat of heresy sneaking into their fellowship. However, it is from the top-heavy, institutional church structures that heresy is more likely to be birthed.[68] Frank Viola is direct

---

61. McLaren 2004, 246.

62. Simson 2009, xv.

63. Vieira 2006, 72.

64. McLaren 2004, 246; Viola and Barna 2008, 120.

65. Rutz 2005, 159.

66. Kimball 2003, 102; Simson 2009, 17 & 50.

67. Rutz 2005, 66.

68. Green 2009, 31.

in countering this thinking, calling it "a charade." Theological error is avoided, not by submitting to a denominational covering, but to the Holy Spirit.[69] He actually sees the denominational system as one that perpetuates heresy, not avoiding it.[70] It is instead the close-knit, mutually edifying community of the small home gathering, notes Matthew Green, that largely protects itself from heretical digressions.[71]

The result of these fellowships is that participants are engaged in a high level of spiritual support, encouragement, and engagement that is not feasible with the larger gathering size of the traditional church.[72] It is not surprising, then, that one of the oft-cited tenets of the house church movement – as well as its cousin, the small group – is that of forming new house churches when the gathering size grows to a level where true community is difficult to maintain, usually around twenty people.[73]

Regarding the possible inference of small groups as a house church alternative, George Barna states that the popular small group/cell group/home fellowships that are propagated by local churches are a *supplemental* activity of which the traditional church is the focus. As such, despite their seeming similarity, they are not included in the house church/simple church discussion.[74]

Much has been written about small groups (such as *Nine Keys to Effective Small Group Leadership* by Carl F. George) and house churches (consider *Mega Shift: Igniting Spiritual Power* by James Rutz), a fuller discussion of which transcends the intent of this work. A plethora of excellent books can be

---

69. Viola 2008, 229-230.

70. Ibid., 235.

71. Green 2009, 31.

72. Rutz 2005, 101.

73. Simson 2009, 3-4 & 156.

74. Barna 2005, 64-65.

consulted for additional explanation of these practices and to garner practical implementation insights (many of which are listed in Appendix E). The possible future potency of this move is perhaps best summed up in *The Rabbit and the Elephant*: "God is changing the heart of the church – transforming her from the inside out – and this change has the potential to be as big as the Reformation."[75]

75. Dale 2009, 197.

THE GREAT EMERGENCE

The timing of this emerging corresponds with Christianity's cycle of 500-year eras that was revealed in Chapter 1. With the Great Reformation marking the beginning of the last semi-millennial movement, the next one is in the works.[1] Phyllis Tickle calls this the Great Emergence,[2] which takes the church's emergence to the next level. "The Great Emergence," Tickle states, "is coalescing" within postmodernism.[3]

At the time of Martin Luther, the societal unit was the fiefdom of the local village. This gradually gave way to the familial unit as the new foundation of society. The resulting shift produced significant societal upheavals that resulted in disorientation and disequilibrium. Fast-forward 500 years to the present, and an analogous transition is transpiring; a parallel transformative shift is taking place, with the nuclear family feeling threatened by alternative "domestic and affinity arrangements" that are appearing both legally and socially.[4]

Another interesting parallel is that the central technological player at the time

---

1. Tickle 2008, Emergence, 27.

2. Ibid., 33, 41.

3. Ibid., 64.

4. McLaren 2004, 11, in the foreword written by Phyllis Tickle; also Tickle 2008, Emergence, 51.

of the Reformation was the printing press.[5] For the people of the Reformation Era, written words fueled their burgeoning movement. On both a personal and societal level, the printed word served first to instigate and then to cultivate their revolution of religious thought and practice.[6] In analogous fashion, the Internet plays an equally or even more pivotal role today in influencing "thought, commerce, and the shaping of positions and decision-making" in the world in which it exists.[7]

Perhaps most striking is that while "the Reformation was the result of a grassroots change in theology by ordinary people having access to scripture in their own language," the parallel change today is that "the church – instead of the Bible – is being put back into the hands of ordinary people."[8] The objections to both of these moves carry an eerily similar alarm: for the former, it is that untrained and unqualified people cannot understand the Bible; for the latter, it is that the laity cannot run a church.[9]

In today's culture, which Diana Butler Bass calls post-Christian and pluralistic, mainline Christianity is becoming increasingly outdated and antiquated.[10] Beginning in the 1960s, Christianity in both North American and Europe moved into "a seeking mode," in which "vast numbers of people have become spiritually

---

5. McLaren 2004, 10, in the foreword written by Phyllis Tickle; also Tickle 2008, Emergence, 53; also Bass 2008, History, 156.

6. Bass 2009, History, 152-153.

7. McLaren 2004, 10, in the foreword written by Phyllis Tickle; also Tickle 2008, Emergence, 53.

8. Dale 2009, 23.

9. Ibid., 23.

10. Bass 2009 History, 23-24 and Bass 2004, 9.

unmoored, moving from one religious opinion to another."[11]

With the aforementioned shift in the societal unit, the birth and explosive growth of the Internet, and an unsettled and nomadic spirituality that arose in recent decades, Tickle contends that the Great Emergence is a direct result of the twentieth century.[12] Citing an effective consensus of opinion among observers, the Great Emergence "will rewrite Christian theology – and thereby American culture – into something far more Jewish, more paradoxical, more narrative, and more mystical than anything the Church has had for the last seventeen or eighteen hundred years," declares Tickle. "There is no question that the Great Emergence is the configuration of Christianity which is in ascendency."[13]

In contemplation of Tickle's writing on this topic, Bass summarizes that "Christianity has entered a new period of reform," which is producing "a global renewal based on...an integration of religious traditions and spiritual insights across the Christian spectrum."[14] This is a move towards unity.

Transcending the current labels of conservative, moderate, and liberal Christianity, Bass notes that an "unexpected renewal" is occurring in North America. It consists of an "energized cluster" of evolving Christians who are being christened as progressive or emerging; the term she prefers is "generative Christianity."[15] All this is occurring at a time when younger generations have an openness to Jesus and what He teaches.[16]

---

11. Ibid., 223.

12. Tickle 2008, Emergence, 74.

13. Ibid., 161-162.

14. Bass 2009, History, 154.

Given this, it is not surprising that many individuals in contemporary society are being driven to find an authentic spirituality, for word and deed to cogently intertwine, and to jettison the phony and the hypocritical facets of modern religion.[17] This emergence is not merely a generational shift, which occurs with predictable regularity as each successive demographic ages and matures. "This is about a complete shift in worldview, about the first major philosophical watershed in four or five centuries," asserts Jones .[18] Succinctly, what is transpiring today is a transformation parallel to that which occurred in the sixteenth century.[19] Like the semi-millennial shifts that preceded it, the Great Emergence represents profound changes in society, politics, economics, intellectualism, and culture. However, unlike its predecessors, its reach is not geographically contained, but global in scope.[20]

A Quadrilateral View

In order to elucidate these developments and provide clarity about the makeup of Christianity today, Tickle recalls a quadrilateral diagram, first advanced in the 1960s, which she updated to reflect the present map of North American Christianity. As the name implies, the quadrilateral consists of four roughly equal sections. The upper left is labeled the "Liturgicals," comprising Roman Catholic, Anglican, Lutheran, Oriental Orthodox, and Eastern Orthodox faiths. Below that, in the lower left are the "Renewalists," which includes the pentecostal movement and their charismatic offshoots. The upper right quadrant is labeled as the "Social Justice Christians," which is the domicile of mainline churches (elsewhere in this work referred to as the "Liberals"). Under that, in the lower

---

17. Bass 2009, History, 155-156.

18. Jones 2008, 68.

19. Ibid., 36.

20. Tickle 2008, Emergence, 120, McLaren 2004, 63.

right sector are the "Conservatives," which over time have also been known as "Evangelicals," "Theocrats," and "Fundamentalists."[21]

It is tempting to attempt to assign every denomination to a specific quadrant of the diagram. While doing so may once have been a simple task, it is no longer the case, with the dividing lines between the sections becoming increasingly equivocal and indistinct.[22] For each quarter, there exists a blurring and overlapping with adjacent sectors;[23] the borders are "semi-permeable."[24] For example, Roman Catholics, while decidedly liturgical, are also great proponents of social justice.[25] The dividing line between the two, albeit indefinite, represents the longstanding tension between faith and works. In similar fashion, the upper quadrant Liturgicals can, at times, be charismatic.[26] Moreover, the "fully charismatic congregations are incorporating forms of ancient liturgy in their worship."[27]

Orthodoxy and Orthopraxy

In general, extending these distinctions to the entire quadrilateral, the horizontal line, which divides the top from the bottom, implies a division between action and belief; that is, orthodoxy versus orthopraxy.[28] Correspondingly, the vertical axis, splitting the left side of the quadrilateral from

---

21. Tickle 2008, Emergence, 125-127.

22. Ibid., 127.

23. Ibid., 129.

24. Ibid., 131.

25. Ibid., 128.

26. Ibid., 129.

27. Ibid., 129.

28. Ibid., 145 & 129-130.

the right, separates orthonomy (employing "aesthetic or harmonic purity as a tool for discerning the truth," be it "doctrine or practice") on the left from theonomy ("only God can be the source of perfection in action and thought") on the right.[29] Tickle pointedly notes that the Quakers are, as a result of their beginnings, residing on this horizontal axis, smartly between the upper right quadrant of the Social Justice Christians and the lower right Conservatives.[30]

The Gathering Center

As this blurring or blending of the once distinct borders between quadrants continued at the close of the twentieth century – especially where the four interior corners meet – a comingling of thought and faith has occurred. Tickle calls this internal area on the quadrilateral "the Gathering Center." This inner core of the diagram represents a "mélange of 'things' cherry-picked from each quadrant and put together – some may say cobbled together – without any original intent and certainly with no design beyond that of conversation." This center represents the Great Emergence; it is "truly post-modern, post-denominational, post-rational, post-Enlightenment, post-literate," and "post-Christendom."[31]

Bass shares the similarly sounding labels that she gleaned from others; these include "postmodern Christianity," "post-traditional religion," and the "end of Christendom."[32] Dan Kimball concurs with the "post-Christian" label, also throwing the phrase "pre-Christian" into the mix.[33] This simultaneous use of the pre- and post- prefix labels confirms that emerging Christians are a comingling of

---

29. Ibid., 149-150.

30. Ibid., 154.

31. Ibid., 131-136.

32. Bass 2009, History, 214-215.

33. Kimball 2007, 27, 73, 200-201, & 205.

the old and the new.[34]

The Outer Edges

As this center of emergence congealed – and continues to do so – a backlash occurred.[35] It was the classic tension of tradition versus change, a war between clinging to the past and adapting, changing, and growing towards an unknown future. Bass states that sometimes the conflict was even "between rival versions of tradition." In addition, there is the added complication that the traditions being fought for are themselves gradually morphing over time.[36] At its core this is essentially a conflict between postmodern and modern.

Postmodern thought is solidifying in the center of the diagram. Those holding tightly to the modern aspects of their faith – that is, their inherited church – are being pushed to the fringes.[37] These folks will, in reaction to the center, seek to maintain the status quo and "aggressively dedicate themselves and their resources to reversing all the changes that had enabled, and [are] continuing to enable, the center and the emergence taking place there."[38] These are the "reacters."[39]

As scholars project this trend into the future, they assign numbers to the diagram, with 60 percent gathering in the center area of emergence, and the "reacters" as 9 to 13 percent, residing in the outside corners of their respective

---

34. Jones 2008, xix.

35. Tickle 2008, Emergence, 136.

36. Bass 2004, 35-36.

37. Tickle 2008, Emergence, 136-139.

38. Ibid., 136-137.

39. Ibid., 139. Though one might opt for the conventional spelling of "reactors," Tickle uses "reacters."

quadrants and clinging to their historical traditions.[40] In a confirming manner, "the Barna Group predicts that by 2025, the local church will lose roughly half of its current 'market share,' and alternative forms of faith experience and expression will pick up the slack."[41] This discussion is graphically summarized in Figure 1. (Note that the diagram is not to scale. Recall that the Gathering Center will comprise 60 percent and the "reacters," 9 to 13 percent, leaving about 30 percent for the space in between.)

Tickle notes that from the Gathering Center the modern house church movement has been quietly birthed.[42]

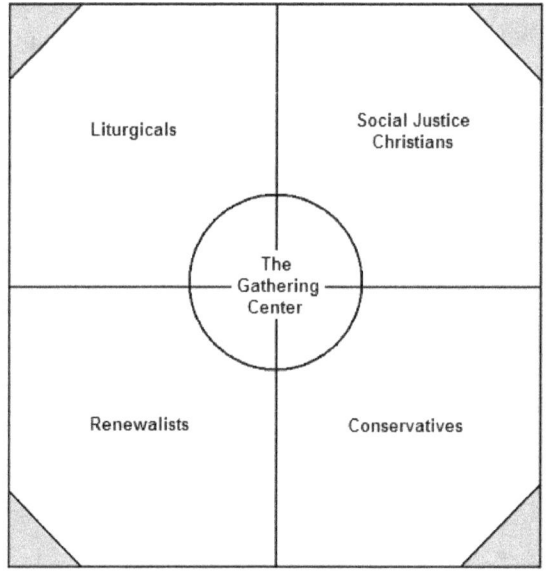

☐ = Backlash - Maintain Status Quo

---

40. Ibid., 139.

41. Dale 2009, 37.

42. Tickle 2008, Emergence, 134.

Figure 1. Overview of the Quadrilateral[43]

The Space Between

The remaining 30 percent or so will exist between these polarizing extremes, forming concentric circles of thought; they are neither emergents nor "reacters," essentially serving as a progression of thought, bridging the space between the emergent and reactionary poles. Proceeding from the outermost circle to the innermost are first the "Traditionalists," then the "Re-traditioning," next the "Progressives," and finally the "Hyphenateds." Like everything else in the diagram, their borders are indistinct, with some degree of overlap.[44]

The first and outermost ring, the "Traditionalists," will be most like the reactionaries residing in the outer corners, who are "keepers of the family faith"; that is, their inherited church. In like manner, the Traditionalists will follow this familial faith, all the while accommodating gradual change.

The second ring is the Re-traditioning. They too will stick to their traditions, while simultaneously working to update and refurbish it.

Close by, almost indistinguishable, are the Progressives. These Christians are not refurbishing their faith; they are remodeling it. They seek to remain within their Reformation-rooted faith communities while adopting postmodern realities.

The last concentric circle, the one closest to the center, is the Hyphenateds. Essentially they will move one step beyond the Progressives, towards the emergent center, while keeping one foot planted in their denominational heritage. The result is a hyphenated designation, such as Presby-emergent, Metho-emergent, Angli-emergent, Luther-emergent, and so forth.

Over time, adherents in these various circles of understanding will migrate between the bands, moving closer either to the reactionary extremes or to the

---

43. Ibid., 137. This is a reproduction of the key elements of Tickle's diagram, which she explains on pages 123 through 139; the diagram is not to scale.

44. Ibid., 140.

emergent center. This emergent center represents a rebirth of Christianity and the next placeholder in history.[45] This portion of the discussion is graphically summarized in Figure 2. (Again, he diagram is not to scale. Recall that the Gathering Center will comprise 60 percent, the "reacters," nine percent, and the space between – the four concentric circles – about 30 percent.)

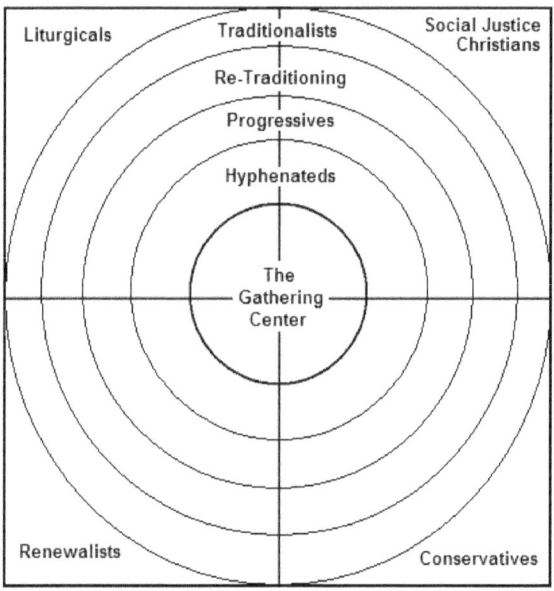

Figure 2. The Currents Between the Gathering Center and the Polarized Extremes[46]

A Three Dimensional Understanding

Diana Butler Bass also points out that society is currently in a transitional

---

45. Ibid., 140-143.

46. Ibid., 140. This is a reproduction of the key elements of Tickle's diagram, which she explains on pages 139 through 144; the diagram is not to scale.

situation – it is moving from one space to another; it is emerging.[47] In her book *The Practicing Congregation: Imagining a New Old Church*, Bass maps things a bit differently, but no less instructively or insightfully. Bass places two continuums of "practice" and "theology" at right angles to produce a two-dimensional grid. She labels the horizontal axis the theological continuum, moving from liberal on the left extreme to conservative on the right. Correspondingly, she labels the vertical axis the practice continuum, placing established church practices (which she elsewhere calls "inherited" practices[48]) at the top of the continuum, moving towards intentionality at the bottom.[49] Bass further characterizes this vertical continuum as one of a birthright religious culture (Established) versus negotiated religious identity (Intentional).[50] The two continuums are illustrated in Figure 3.

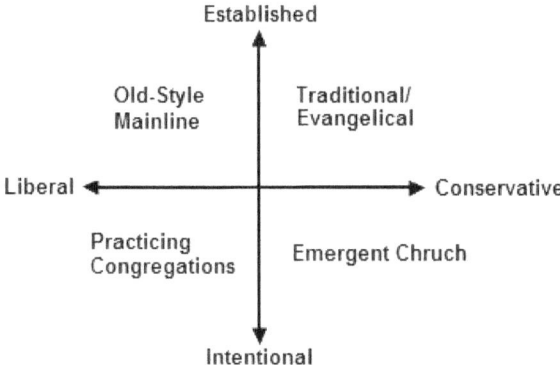

Figure 3. The Theological and Practice Continuums, mapped at right

---

47. Bass 2007.

48. Ibid.

49. Bass 2004, 84 (chart); 74-84 (description).

50. Bass 2007.

angles[51]

In the resulting four quadrants, Bass notes four congregational types. In the upper left, which is the Established-Liberal sector, resides Old-Style Mainline. Next to that, in the upper right (the Established-Conservative quadrant) are the Traditional/Evangelicals. On the lower left of the grid, which is the Intentional-Liberal area, are the Practicing Congregations. Next to them in the lower right corner (the Intentional-Conservative block) is the Emergent Church.[52]

In this chart, Bass relegates the Emergent Church as a product exclusively of evangelicals. However, the other sources cited in this work employ a broader view of emergence, seeing it as evolving out of mainline as well. Although a distinction is made in the labeling, the resulting conclusions are consistent. This can be confirmed in her characterization of intentional congregations, which sound emergent: "The primary model for intentional congregations is faith-as-pilgrimage, a dynamic and organic image of mobility and change while fixing on an ultimate destination – union with God."[53] She later muses that "eventually, perhaps inevitably, people from either side would meet."[54]

Bass notes that the liberal-conservative divide is in actuality a product of late modernity. Therefore, movements into postmodernity blur this polarized divide, as do movements towards intentionality. In short, with intentionality amid postmodernity, there is more commonality on the theological continuum; a consensus converges. For the liberals, she calls this move "postliberalism," which is not to suggest an "intellectual conversion to conservatism." Correspondingly,

---

51. Bass 2004, 84. This is a reproduction of the key elements of Bass's diagram, which she explains on pages 74 through 84.

52. Ibid., 84.

53. Ibid., 81.

54. Ibid., 86-87.

for the conservative camp, she calls this move "postevangelicalism," which likewise is not a conversion to liberalism.[55]

This begs for a third dimension to be added to the model; a z-axis, portraying a continuum of worldview – that is, how reality is interpreted – marking movement from pre-modern to modern to postmodern. Emanating from the two-dimensional model at the points of postliberal and postevangelical, the z dimension jumps off the page to construct a multilayered model. This axis, she states, is quite possibly moving into a "New Reformation." To help illustrate the relationship between the x and z axis, Bass uses as an example the dispute about gay ordination. She notes that this is not really a debate between liberal and conservative, but actually one of modern versus postmodern.[56]

The greater the movement into postmodernity, the greater the possibility that the distinctions of liberal and conservative will disappear, possibly converging into a single, unified perspective. This is a logical conclusion, given that the liberal and conservative mindsets are dependent on a modern worldview. Consistent with this model, the established church institutions are holding their congregations in modernism, thereby perpetuating this liberal-conservative dualism. Conversely, moving into postmodernism lessens this dichotomy and fosters an environment for increased unity.[57] In looking at the trajectory of developments of this nature, Jim Wallis sees "a rapidly expanding *new denomination*" consisting of a growing group of those claiming to be "*spiritual but not religious.*"[58]

"I believe that we are witnessing a new reformation that is transforming the way Christianity will be experienced in the new millennium," opines Donald E.

---

55. Ibid., 85-86.

56. Bass 2004, 87 and Bass 2007.

57. Bass 2007.

58. Wallis 2008, 16, italics are added to indicate text that Wallis put in quotes.

Miller.[59] Unlike the Reformation of Martin Luther's day, this one will not be about confronting doctrine but instead challenging "the medium through which the message of Christianity is articulated."[60] Calling them "new paradigm" churches, they, like "upstart religious groups of the past," jettison much of the established religious status quo in the process. This includes "creating a new genre of worship music, restructuring the organizational character of institutional religion, and democratizing access" by restoring "the Protestant principle of the priesthood of all believers."[61] Exemplifying this new paradigm, Phyllis Tickle cites The Vineyard, Calvary Chapels, and Hope Chapels. Interestingly, it is the Association of Vineyard Churches that may be one of the few examples of a traditionally configured expression of emergent Christianity.[62]

---

59. Donald E. Miller, "Rethinking Church: Learning from new paradigm congregations,"
   http://www.thunderstruck.org/holysmoke/rethinkingchurch.htm
   (accessed February 6, 2010), 1.

60. Ibid., 1.

61. Ibid., 1.

62. Tickle 2008, Emergence, 156-157.

Going Forward: A Requisite Theological Shift

Postmodernism, through its predilection towards tolerance and diversification, is providing a societal shift that is open to embrace cultural unity. Likewise, in emergence – which is springing from postmodernism – is a corresponding spiritual shift towards greater Christian unity. A recurring theme within emergence is new ways of understanding and embracing the Holy Spirit.[1]

Embedded within emergence, then, is a theological shift that needs to be intentionally pursued by all Christians in order to move towards the realization of Jesus' prayer for unity. It is adopting a more balanced Trinitarian comprehension and pursuit of God. In doing so, diverse Christian theological perspectives can converge into a unified point of understanding and acceptance.

According to Frank Viola and George Barna, Christian unity does not have as its basis an organizational structure or doctrinal statement; it is organic in nature, as manifested by the reality of the communion and community of the Father, Son, and Holy Spirit. In other words, unity is Trinitarian.[2] The Trinity is "three persons in one essence." This is a Western Christianity (Roman Catholic and Protestant) understanding. However, Eastern Orthodox adherents are also Trinitarian, stating that "the one true God has always existed as God the Father, God the Son, and God the Holy Spirit."[3]

---

1. Bass 2006, 242.

2. Viola 2008, 128.

3. Wagner 2004, 157-158.

Reclaiming the Holy Spirit

Tony Jones boldly asserts that most American Christians today, despite claiming allegiance to the doctrine of the Trinity, don't in practice acknowledge the reality of the Holy Spirit; their reliance on Him is nonexistent. Although embracing the Father and the Son, they dismiss or even ignore the existence and work of the Spirit; they are functionally binitarian instead of Trinitarian, which Parker Palmer labels as "functional atheism."[4]

With the effective jettisoning of the Holy Spirit, the practical conclusion is that it is up to the church to grow itself. "When the church places undue emphasis on its programs, buildings, staffing, or other human inventions, reliance on the Holy Spirit has most likely been lost," Jones adds. What started as "self-centeredness expands via institutionalism." He concludes by declaring, "A return to true Trinitarianism in the American church is desperately needed."[5] This tracks with emergent Dispatch 18, affirming the place and power of the spirit of God.[6]

It is noteworthy that many emergent followers of Jesus speak freely and fondly of the mysterious work of the Holy Spirit in their spiritual pilgrimage. To them, accepting and agreeing with the moving acts of the Holy Spirit embodies the concept of doing things differently. It is therefore not surprising that emergents have a predilection to embrace change; they see it as an integral and inseparable part of their spiritual transformation and growth.[7]

Tickle states that approximately one-fourth of the emergent/emerging movement have a charismatic mindset, be it by heritage or affinity. As such, they carry with them a "central belief in the Holy Spirit as authority" into their

---

4. Jones 2008, 201-202.

5. Ibid., 203.

6. Ibid., 202.

7. Bass 2006, 242.

emerging proclivities.[8] Emergence, she continues, is moving "toward a system of ecclesial authority that waits on the Spirit and rests on the interlacing lives of Bible-listening, Bible-honoring believers."[9]

As discussed earlier, one such emergent manifestation is open fellowships such as house churches. At their meetings, participants "include the Holy Spirit – as the Master of Ceremonies, not just the Guest of Honor,"[10] notes James Rutz. In like manner, Viola and Barna quip, "Isn't the Holy Spirit supposed to lead all of our church meetings?"[11]

This burgeoning elevation of the Holy Spirit, although a recent development, was prophetically foretold several centuries ago. The fulfillment of this prophecy is currently unfolding. As covered in Chapter 1, Phyllis Tickle dubs the Great Emergence as the latest installment of "a semi-millennial upheaval." She further notes that it is also part of "a bi-millennial phenomenon." From the perspective of medieval Christendom, as exemplified by Joachim of Fiore, history is prophetically divided into three eras, each lasting two thousand years. There is the past age of the Father, with a "primary emphasis of God the Father" (circa 2000 to 0 BCE), the present age of the Son, with a "primary emphasis on God the Son" (circa 0 to 2000 CE), and a future third age of the Spirit, with "the primacy in worship and in human affairs of God the Spirit" (circa 2000 to 4000 CE). While medieval man saw the age of the spirit as future, today's Christians are able to experience it as the nascent present.[12]

These two timelines – one semi-millennial and the other bimillennial – are presently intersecting, with the merging of a 500-year historic cycle and a

---

8. Tickle 2008, Emergence, 85.

9. Ibid., 153.

10. Rutz 2005, 101.

11. Viola and Barna 2008, 72.

12. Tickle 2008, Emergence, 164-165.

2000-year prophetic cycle. The result is an intermingling of the Great Emergence with the age of the Holy Spirit.[13] The church, notes George Barna, is "being restored so the Holy Spirit can work effectively through the body of Christ."[14]

Effectively concurring, C. Peter Wagner states that what is presently manifesting is another radical shift in Christian thought and practice. He likewise adds that it is on the order of a magnitude not seen since the Protestant Reformation. However, in truth it is arguably a more radical and significant development. While leaving essential doctrines intact – such as "the authority of Scripture, justification by faith, and the priesthood of believers" – the change (which Wagner calls "the new apostolic reformation") is reengineering how churches function and operate. The possible labels he cites for this movement include "new churches," "ChurchNext," "new paradigm churches," and "postdenominational churches."[15]

Although new movements of the Holy Spirit are the underlying catalyst for this new apostolic reformation, it is not exclusively charismatic, with an estimated 20 percent of the movement being comprised of noncharismatic evangelicals.[16] This form of Christianity, which is focused on the work and movement of the Holy Spirit, is the fastest growing segment of Christianity, the only one growing faster than Islam.[17] The foundational basis for this is the pentecostal and charismatic movements that were birthed and matured during the past century.

The Pentecostal and Charismatic Movements

---

13. Tickle 2008, Emergence, 164-165; Bass 2006, 242 and 320, footnote.

14. Barna 2005, 103.

15. Wagner 2004, 10.

16. Ibid., 11.

17. Ibid., 15.

Volumes have been written on the pentecostal movement, as well as the broader charismatic movement that followed it some five decades later. For the purpose of this work, even though a brief overview will be provided, the details are not germane. The focus is on the *outcome* of these movements – that is, their effects on the greater Christian body and the implications they offer in pursuing church unity through a truly Trinitarian understanding.

While the Holy Spirit was active and moving in the early church, modernism has effectively relegated Him to a secondary or even inconsequential role. This began to change with the pentecostal movement. The origins of the pentecostal revival date back to Kansas in 1901, and it was brought to the forefront a few years later (1906 through 1909) in Los Angeles with the Azusa Street revival. The principal teaching of the then burgeoning movement was "that every Christian must be anointed by the Holy Spirit [to] do the supernatural work of Christ."[18]

The Azusa Street revival laid the groundwork for the greater charismatic movement some fifty years later. It was Episcopal priest Dennis Bennett who is often cited as the father of the modern charismatic movement. In 1960 he publically declared to his congregation his baptism by the Holy Spirit. This admission was both surprising and controversial, ultimately resulting in calls for his resignation, his subsequent move to a different congregation, and his founding of the Christian Renewal Association.[19] He later wrote that he understood the Holy Spirit's baptism as analogous to a car's drivetrain, which transfers power from the engine to the wheels. While it is evangelism – implicitly Jesus – that starts the engine, it is the Holy Spirit that makes the car move.[20]

Despite making an implicit connection between evangelism and the charismatic movement, Bennett adamantly asserted that "charismatic renewal

---

18. Grady 2010, Holy Spirit, 41-42.

19. Dennis Bennett, "God's Strength for This Generation," Sojourners (April 2010): 55, from the introduction by unnamed editors.

20. Bennett, 2010, 55.

is not an evangelical renewal," even though the former serves to fuel the latter. The church's essential task, he maintained, is not about teaching or preaching, but must be charismatic, "manifesting the gifts and fruit of the Spirit," thereby pointing to Jesus' active work today. "This," he insists, "is a breaking forth of the Holy Spirit from the religious prison in which He has been confined through much of Christian history."[21]

Although Bennett was likely not the first mainline pastor to be baptized by the Holy Spirit, he was arguably the first to openly proclaim and publically promote it. Within a few short years, adherents in nearly every Protestant denomination and tradition were likewise experiencing the Holy Spirit's baptism. Today, the fastest growing segment of Christianity is the charismatics, who are approximately 640 million strong and comprise one-third of all Christians globally.[22] The Reverend Bill Wilson predicts that the present "generation is positioned not only to see the [charismatic] movement grow, but [to] really experience the Holy Spirit in a totally new dimension."[23]

David Neff writes that what "made the charismatic renewal remarkable was the ecumenical fellowship that it created." This ecumenical mindset emanates from the realization that the Holy Spirit is "animating and transforming others."[24]

Although it can scarcely be identified as a movement at this point, over its fifty-year history the charismatic perspective has served as an example, effectively changing the manner and form of how most churches understand and worship God. It also resulted in the rapid and remarkable proliferation of charismatic Christianity worldwide.[25]

---

21. Ibid., 56.

22. Anderson 2010, 16; Yung 2010, 32.

23. Anderson 2010, 17.

24. David Neff, "Ardor and Order," Christianity Today (May 2010), 53.

25. Ibid., 53.

A Historical Timeline

For the sake of clarity and increased understanding, the pentecostal and charismatic movements are historically divided into three eras. The "third wave" of the Holy Spirit is an expression coined by C. Peter Wagner,[26] evoking an awareness of three historical segments of the Holy Spirit's activity in the twentieth century. The Azusa Street revival marked the first wave of the Holy Spirit, birthing the pentecostal movement and fueling its proliferation over the next fifty years. In 1960, the second wave of Holy Spirit activity burst onto the scene, with the pentecostal movement transcending its borders and spreading throughout many other Protestant denominations and the Roman Catholic Church; this marked the birth of the greater charismatic movement. The third wave originated in the 1980s, with a renaissance in church planting and manifestations of signs and wonders within evangelistic efforts.

Accompanying each wave was a subtle shift in the theological understanding of the Holy Spirit. With the first wave came the assertion that the baptism of the Holy Spirit is subsequent to conversion and marked by a separate event. It is evidenced by speaking in tongues, which was a staunch requirement for validation.

The second wave continued with the understanding of a second and subsequent baptism or filling of the Holy Spirit. However, it was also more accepting of the reality that all Christians have, to some extent, the Holy Spirit present in them and at work through them. The manifestation of speaking in tongues was downgraded from a prerequisite to normative, but it was no longer a necessary evidentiary expectation.

With the third wave came the identification of Spirit baptism as part of the conversion experience, as opposed to a second, subsequent event. Speaking in tongues may not be emphasized in this wave and the practice may not even be

---

26. Wagner, 2004, 43.

a typical aspect of public charismatic meetings. In fact, some third wave leaders do not possess this gift.[27]

Although Bennett figured prominently into the formation of the second wave, he dismissed Wagner's third wave, insisting that the baptism of the Holy Spirit is separate from salvation and that speaking in tongues is a required manifestation. He saw notions to the contrary as an accommodation for those who did not speak in tongues and who lacked a comprehension of the true charismatic renewal. This assertion was made circa 1990.[28] Bennett died in 1991.[29] It is noteworthy that the third wave was in its infancy at the time of his pronouncement. One is left to ponder if his views might have moderated in the subsequent twenty years.

Despite Wagner's identification of the third wave of the Holy Spirit that promotes a less doctrinarian and more inclusive embrace of the Holy Spirit's activity in today's church, there are those like Bennett who adhere to a narrower and more exclusive understanding. Regardless of the degree of advocacy, the result is two groups of Christians: those who welcome the Holy Spirit and those who in actual practice ignore or minimize Him. What varies is the degree of alignment with or alienation from the person and power of the Holy Spirit.

Regarding this division between charismatic and non-charismatic Christians, J. Lee Grady believes that a meaningful reconciliation is possible, but that it "will require loving acceptance and understanding on both sides."[30] Interestingly, it was Bennett who sought to defuse the polarization, writing that those who are baptized by the Holy Spirit should not understand it as a sign of spiritual maturity, favor, or superiority. It is merely a new dimension of their Christian journey in which they can either progress or regress. Bennett's sage

---

27. http://en.wikipedia.org/wiki/Third_Wave_of_the_Holy_Spirit, accessed, 2/6/2010.

28. Bennett 2010, 56.

29. http://en.wikipedia.org/wiki/Dennis_Bennett, accessed 3/7/2011.

30. Grady 2010, Holy Spirit, 192.

recommendation is for charismatics to seek and pray for a humble spirit. Grady succinctly summarized this perspective, stating that too many charismatics developed a spiritual pride after encountering Holy Spirit baptism."[31]

Although the traditional theology of the pentecostal and charismatic camps dictates that speaking in tongues is a required evidentiary experience, there has been a moderation of that staunchly adamant position. This is accelerated by the present reality that in some pentecostal churches a majority has not received the gift of speaking in tongues. This reality is serving to mitigate the dichotomous schism between those who have and those who have not spoken in tongues.[32]

Two thousand years ago, the church in Corinth seemingly struggled with this same divisive issue over spiritual gifts. Paul devoted space to address this in his first letter to them, declaring that a diversity of gifts is needed for the church body to function properly. He indicated that it is God who determines and organizes the allotment of the various gifts of the church (1 Corinthians 12:17-21).

Paul did not elevate speaking in tongues as an indication of spiritual superiority. With this in mind, Grady recommends that those in the charismatic camp – of which he is a part – must free themselves from their spiritual pride, accepting as fact that not all Christians speak in tongues, just as Paul stated (1 Corinthians 12:28-30). Conversely, Grady says it is imperative to accept other Christians as likewise gifted, albeit in other but equally legitimate ways.[33]

In a corresponding manner, the non-charismatics must embrace a more moderate stance, accepting Christians who speak in tongues and exercise spiritual gifts. It is imperative to recall the words of Paul, who firmly stated, "Do not forbid speaking in tongues" (1 Corinthians 14:39). Grady adds that the fundamental and conservative evangelical factions of Christendom who adhere to a dispensational stance that some of the Holy Spirit's activities were only

---

31. Ibid., 192.

32. Ibid., 191.

33. Ibid., 193.

functional in the early church must not reject charismatic Christians, label them as ignorant, or call them theologically misguided. They are not a deviant group on the fringe that has departed from orthodox belief.[34]

Both groups, Grady hopes, will moderate their divisive stances, moving towards an accepting middle ground. There must be an acknowledgment that the Holy Spirit is alive and active in the present day, while at the same time allowing that specific spiritual gifts are not a requisite salvation requirement. Each party can and should bring something useful to the greater whole.[35] As Paul stated, "There are many parts, but one body" (1 Corinthians 12:20). This move can be aptly aided by adopting a balanced Trinitarian perspective.

Balanced Trinitarianism

Christian A. Schwarz, in his concise booklet, *The Threefold Art of Experiencing God: The Liberating Power of a Trinitarian Faith*, writes that there is a prevalent deficit in Christians' comprehension of the Trinitarian nature of God. Schwarz states that this lack of awareness and appreciation for God's existence and revelation as a threefold entity is the source of an appalling paralysis for much of Christendom, creating conflicts and divisions that result in much disunity.[36]

By fully understanding and completely embracing the Trinity in a different manner – which is in actuality reclaiming it from the past – Christians are able to view the Godhead from a fresh perspective, thereby experiencing God in a new way – at least one that is new to them. The result, Schwarz asserts, leads to a fuller and greater appreciation of personal and denominational strengths, weaknesses, limitations, adversarial perceptions, dreams, and fears. This newfound comprehension sheds illuminating light on the sources of

---

34. Ibid., 193.

35. Ibid., 194.

36. Schwarz 1999, 4.

much church conflict and the unseen foundational impetus that propels and
perpetuates them. With this knowledge, then, comes a requisite understanding
that is needed to usher in a movement towards constructive change and a
reclamation of church unity by embracing a holistic, Trinitarian view of God.[37]

Although many view the doctrine of the Trinity as a dry and abstract theology,
Schwarz asserts "that it is the most practical theological topic" he knows. The key
is to free God as a three-in-one reality, releasing Him from Trinitarian abstractions
and theological formulations. The result of this liberation is to unleash an
"explosive power" that possesses the potential to completely transform followers
of Jesus on both a personal and corporate level. Adopting and maintaining a
holistic view of the Trinitarian nature of God is one of the key underpinnings
of Christianity.[38]

It is noteworthy that when the elemental roots of the church are fully attended
to – including a balanced Trinitarian view – organic church growth is a normative
and automatic result. (The phrase "organic church" is used here in a descriptive
manner and is not to be confused with the label "organic church" as employed in
the earlier house church discussion.) In this regard, summarizing the main insight
from his book entitled *Natural Church Development*, Schwarz writes that when
quality is pursued, quantity is the result.[39]

Schwarz acknowledges that people perceive God in various ways, but without
the dimension of experience, it is impossible to comprehend the Christian faith.
God, therefore, can only be encountered via one's relationship to Him. Since
God exists as three interconnected entities – Father, Son, and Holy Spirit –
the potential exists for individuals to likewise experience Him in three ways,
in a Trinitarian, threefold manner. Just as a prism allows for the perception
of different colors of light, the parts of the Trinity allow for the perception of

---

37. Ibid., 4.

38. Ibid., 5.

39. Ibid., 4-5.

different facets of God, and each has unique beauty.[40]

Comprehending the Godhead

The common labels for the members of the Trinity are Father, Son, and Holy Spirit; these serve to express the interpersonal relationships of the three-in-one Godhead. In his elucidation, Schwarz instead opts for designations that reflect God's relationship to mankind, using the respective labels of Creator, Jesus, and Spirit. Each of these three revelations of God not only portrays something of God Himself, but also reveals a different aspect of His character. These are a "creation revelation," a "salvation revelation," and a "personal revelation." Each revelation is aimed at establishing an aspect of the relationship between God and his followers. Although each of these revelations points to the same God, each provides a different – albeit incomplete – means of encounter. Therefore, whenever "one of the three dimensions is neglected, we have a partial and imperfect experience with God." This points to the source of most problems within the church today: "an incomplete understanding of the threefold revelation of God."[41]

Just as the Godhead is expressed interpersonally in three ways, as Father, Son, and Holy Spirit, and is revealed to mankind as Creator, Jesus, and Spirit, there are several other Trinitarian understandings. First, there are the resulting three works of God: creation, salvation, and sanctification. Next, there are three matching manners of being: God "above us," God "among us," and God "in us." Then there are three corresponding forms of how God addresses mankind: "You shall," "You may," and "You can." There are also three complementary levels of His reality: nature, history, and existence. These are followed by three correlated covenants: the Noah covenant (showing God's power over nature), the Sinai covenant (expressing God's power over history), and the Abraham covenant (documenting God's promise for those who believe). Lastly, there

---

40. Ibid., 6-7.

41. Ibid., 8-9.

are three respective sources of knowledge: science, the Bible, and personal experience.[42] Regardless of each distinction or delineation in the preceding triads of perspective, it is the same God that is being revealed and encountered.[43] These perceptions of God via the parts of the Trinity are summarized in Table 1.[44]

Table 1. A Trinitarian Understanding of God

Common Label:	Father	Son	Holy Spirit
Relationship to Mankind:	Creator	Jesus	Spirit
Revelations:	Creation	Salvation	Personal
Works of God:	Creation	Salvation	Sanctification
Manners of Being:	God "above us"	God "among us"	God "in us"
Forms of Addresses:	"You shall"	"You may"	"You can"
Levels of Reality:	Nature	History	Existence
Covenants:	Noah Covenant (over nature)	Sinai Covenant (over history)	Abraham Covenant (for all who believe)
Sources of Knowledge:	Science	Bible	Personal Experience

Three Persons – Three Factions

In the fourth century, Constantine initiated a church council in Nicea. It was there that the doctrine of the Trinity took shape and emerged. It stated that God is one substance but three persons, a doctrine that remains largely intact to this day.

Unfortunately, in focusing on and considering only the three persons portion of this statement, the inescapable conclusion of tritheism results:[45] "The belief that the Father, Son, and Holy Spirit are three separate and distinct gods, heretical

---

42. Ibid., 10-11.

43. Ibid., 12.

44. Ibid., 8-11.

45. Ibid., 12-13.

in orthodox Christianity."[46] This assertion of Christian tritheism may appall many adherents. However, both Jews and Muslims, viewing Christianity as outside observers, do indeed perceive Christianity as a tritheistic (or polytheistic) religion. This is flagrantly supported by Christian proclamations and practices regarding individual parts of the Trinity.[47] From this vantage point, it is only one small step to allow each Christian the option of choosing a "favorite God" from this Christian pantheon – the Father, the Son, or the Holy Spirit.[48]

Once God is viewed in one of these three ways, the means of experiencing Him is diminished by two-thirds. Schwarz states that this is the tragedy that confronts Christians today. The result is that worldwide, Christianity is essentially divided into three factions, each effectively aligning with a different member of the Trinity and the associated revelation of that member of the Godhead.

The group with the label of "liberal" supports the creation revelation, the "evangelical" group supports the salvation revelation, and the "charismatic" group supports the personal revelation. In doing so, various positive and negative connotations are ascribed to each schism, based on their perspective and theological alignment.[49]

Interestingly, shoving emotionally laden rhetoric aside and considering the source meaning of these labels, their original intent can be reclaimed. Liberal suggests liberation or freedom; evangelical, good news or gospel; and charismatic, grace. Freedom, gospel, and grace are three central Christian themes with which no one can reasonably disagree, yet each camp is routinely vilified and criticized by the other two groups.

Consider that liberals focus on biblical themes such as peace, justice, preserving

---

46. The Free Dictionary. http://www.thefreedictionary.com/tritheism, accessed July 26, 2012.

47. Bass 2009, History, 123; Wagner 2004, 160.

48. Schwarz 1999, 12-13.

49. Ibid., 14.

God's creation, and political action; they emphasize sensuality, art, liturgy, and science. Evangelicals stress a personal relationship with Jesus and saving the lost. Charismatics favor experiencing the power of the Holy Spirit and His life-changing power for daily living. These are all correct and good, but problems occur when, with a unilateral focus on a solitary segment of the Godhead, one group isolates itself from the other two. Conflict and division ensue.[50]

Dismissing Two-Thirds

With a singular focus on one "person" of the Trinity, the other two members of the Godhead become relegated to second-class status or, even worse, ignored altogether. The result is that heresy tends to emerge. For liberals the focus is on creation; the threatening heretical view is the adoption of syncretism (the fusion of differing religious systems[51]), since creation is interreligious. For evangelicals, finding the right doctrine about Jesus is the aim, even to the heretical extreme of seeking the discovery of the right theology superseding a personal relationship with Him; the result is dogmatism (proclaiming opinion as fact[52]). For charismatics, the risk is that personal experience can trump Scripture, with the heretical result being spiritualism ("any doctrine...that prefers the spiritual to the material"[53]).[54]

While a common response to this is additional isolation and a further withdrawing from the other two camps, the unfortunate result of doing so is greater disunity and division in Christendom. In order to avoid these respective

---

50. Ibid., 14-15.

51. http://www.thefreedictionary.com/syncretism, accessed March 13, 2010.

52. Ibid.

53. http://www.thefreedictionary.com/spiritualismm, accessed January 26, 2011.

54. Schwarz 1999, 16-17.

heresies, Schwarz prescribes a solution of pursuing and embracing a balanced understanding of the Trinity, equally affirming each of the three aspects and their associated characteristics. The true focus then becomes one God, not three persons.[55] These three factions and their resultant characteristics are summarized in Table 2.[56]

Table 2. Three Factions of Christianity

Member of the Godhead:	Creator	Jesus	Spirit
Factions:	Liberal	Evangelical	Charismatic
Original Intent:	Freedom	Good News	Grace
Common Focus:	Peace, Justice, Creation Care, Political Action, Sensuality, Art, Liturgy, Science	Relationship with Jesus, Saving the Lost	Experiencing the Holy Spirit, Power for Living
Push:	Creation	Right Doctrine	Personal Experience
Risk or Threat:	Syncretism	Dogmatism	Spiritualism

Noting that "a cord of three strands is not quickly broken" (Ecclesiastes 4:12), a prophetic word was given by Dick Mills when he called C. Peter Wagner "to bring together three cords" so that God can "weave [them] into a pattern to accomplish His purposes in the years to come." These three cords correlate with the three major divisions of Protestantism, resulting from the tritheistic pursuit of God and identified as "the *conservative evangelicals*, the *charismatics*, and the *conscientious liberals*."[57]

An interesting twist on this is that sometimes individuals pursue two of these three perspectives while diminishing the third. This results in a trio of dual combinations. One is a liberal-evangelical view, which embraces the Father

---

55. Ibid., 17.

56. Ibid., 12-17.

57. C. Peter Wagner, Warfare Prayer (Ventura, CA: Regal Books, 1992), 40-41; the author's italicized emphasis is retained in the citation.

and the Son. (In this regard, recall Tony Jones's aforementioned charge of a "binitarian" theology in America today, which focuses on the Father and Son, along with the effective dismissal of the Holy Spirit.) The second is an evangelical-charismatic view that highlights the Son and the Spirit, while the third is a charismatic-liberal view, centering on the Spirit and the Father. While not as divisive as a singular pursuit, each of these perspectives are effectively of a twin Godhead that still stops short of a balanced Trinitarian view and the unity that can be realized as a result. The only viable response is embracing, in equality, all three members of the Trinity in a harmonious, one God manner.[58]

A Balanced Understanding of God as Trinity Promotes Unity

As each faction of Christianity embraces a balanced understanding of God, truly and in totality as Trinity, the result is a mutual migration towards the central core of Christianity.[59] In this regard, recall Phyllis Tickle's aforementioned "the Gathering Center" in her quadrilateral view of Christianity in the world today.

"More and more leaders," notes Wagner, "are being moved powerfully by the Holy Spirit to see themselves not primarily as charismatics, Pentecostals, evangelicals, or liberals, but as members of the Body of Christ."[60] Divisive discord and disagreements melt away as irrelevant when the practical pursuit of God coalesces into a unified comprehension of who He is, worshiping and serving Him – not as one part of three – but as one God with three equal and complementing facets. The relentless pursuit and open-minded adoption of a balanced Trinitarian perspective then serves to unite disparate Christian factions into one integrated church, realizing unity,[61] just as Jesus prayed (John 17:20-23).

---

58. Schwarz 1999, 18-19.

59. Ibid., 17.

60. Wagner 1992, 170.

61. Schwarz 1999, 17-19.

CHAPTER SUMMARY

Observing a history of significant semi-millennial shifts – with the last one being the Great Reformation – Phyllis Tickle notes that the next transition is in progress: the Great Emergence. With the Great Emergence, Tickle takes the emergent movement and emerging church – which are birthed from and bathed in a postmodern mindset – to the next level, a greater level. These emerging forms of Christian thought and practice are transcending denominational boundaries and bridging historical, manmade church divisions.

A reoccurring theme within this development is the prominent role of the Holy Spirit. As such, the inevitability of emergence – and the Christian unity that it portends – can be effectively advanced by more fully embracing the Holy Spirit as a viable and equal part of the Trinity and pursuing a balanced Trinitarian comprehension and observance of the Godhead. This will produce a convergence of Christian perspectives, resulting in greater church unity.

CHAPTER 5: CONCLUSIONS

An intersection of key events is presently occurring throughout the world today. These provide a foundation upon which increased Christian unity can be built and realized. Further, this hope for unity can be aptly aided by a coalescence of faith practices in which the Christian Godhead is fully and truly pursued in a balanced Trinitarian manner, where God the Father, God the Savior, and God the Spirit are approached and comprehended in equality.

Research Thesis

Postmodernism, in general, and the resulting new forms of church expressions advocated by postmodern-thinking Christians, specifically, can provide the basis for increased unity in Jesus.

FOCUS STATEMENTS

Three focus statements serve as the overarching structure to this study:

1. To explore what the Bible says about unity for the followers of Jesus.

2. To examine postmodernism's attitudes toward tolerance and acceptance of divergent views.

3. To investigate the reaction of postmodern-thinking Christians to the historical divisions within the church.

IMPLICATIONS OF FINDINGS

Jesus the Christ, as the focal point of the Christian faith and the pivotal player in the history of God's unfolding interaction with His people, serves as teacher, example, and inspiration. Everything He did was intentional, packed with purpose and meaning. It is no wonder that His followers have carefully scrutinized His every recorded action, word, and deed for clues on how to better follow, serve, and worship Him. With this in mind, careful attention to His final moments on earth serve to give a heightened awareness of what was ultimately important to Him, the One who is the most significant individual throughout all history.

With this in mind, consider that, of all the things that Jesus could have done in His final moments on earth before his arrest, He chose to pray. He did not rest for the ordeal ahead, give final instructions to His fickle followers, or offer a loving good-bye to His family and friends. He prayed.

In this prayer, after a brief introductory request that His Father be glorified through what was about to happen, of all the things that Jesus could have addressed, He focused on His followers. He did not request to be spared the ordeal that awaited Him, that His time of suffering would be shortened, that He would have the physical, mental, emotional, and spiritual strength to endure it, or that He would miraculously feel no pain. Instead, He focused on His followers, both present and future.

Of all the things with which He could have concluded His prayer with, Jesus' final, and therefore arguably most important, request was a succinct plea for "complete unity" among His followers (John 17:23). The stated purpose of this unity was that as many individuals as possible would know the Father and His love. Disunity among those who profess to follow Him, Jesus realized, would be the single biggest obstacle that would keep others from knowing the Father (John 17:1-26).

As the New Testament records, the unity for which Jesus prayed and yearned was largely realized by His immediate followers. Although there were most assuredly conflicts and disagreements that led to temporary disunity in the early church, these were not the norm and, as far as can be ascertained from the biblical record, they were in almost all cases effectively dealt with and overcome. Jesus' prayer for the unity of His early followers was largely realized.

A 500-Year Historic Cycle

However, this critical unity for which Jesus prayed was increasingly not the case for His followers in succeeding generations. In the centuries following His death, resurrection, and ascension, His followers had a series of major divisive disagreements. These significant divisional splits began with the withdrawal of Oriental Christianity (during the fifth century) and Eastern (Greek) Orthodoxy later followed (circa 1054). This left the Roman Catholic Church as a third major faction of Christendom. These two splits, separated by five centuries, resulted in three divergent streams of Christianity, not communicating with each other, isolated, and internally focused. A fourth divergence was brewing.

The modern era (circa the 1500s) ushered in with it, among other things, the Reformation (historically pinned to Martin Luther in 1517). Serious doctrinal corrections were needed in the Roman Catholic Church at that time – many of which were later realized. Efforts to address these issues resulted in yet another division, which birthed Protestantism. Notably, this schism occurred roughly 500 years after the last major split within Christendom, continuing a 500-year cycle of episodic change and upheaval.

These protests against the Roman Catholic Church of the day provided the impetus for even greater disunity. Although the protestors agreed that change was warranted, there was seemingly little agreement on the type, scope, and degree of the change. These reformers, while united in purpose, exhibited disunity in their execution. Different streams of reformation resulted.

Another product of modernity, as exemplified by the Enlightenment – also called The Age of Reason – was the elevation of logic and analytical thought. Reason reigned supreme. As this philosophical perspective infiltrated and then influenced the Christian church, it had a wide and deep-reaching effect. While the ancients and pre-modern people viewed everything in life as spiritual, modernity separated and then segregated the spiritual, effectively relegating spiritual matters to the church on Sunday morning. The rest of life, relying on the empirical, was decidedly non-spiritual, which is to say, secular.

In the process, the Holy Spirit's role was also reconsidered. His intangible existence was thrown into question by modernity's penchant for – nay, insistence on – observational confirmation, while His work and influence was likewise eschewed. The Holy Spirit was, at best, diminished and, at worst, dismissed by the modern mindset. Furthermore, modernity postulated that reason and logic would allow mankind to zero in on a singular understanding of truth. This would be the inevitable result from pursuing a progressive path of intellectual iterations geared towards determining an ultimate, unified knowledge.

However, modernity's influence laid the foundation within the Christian church for more movement towards greater disunity. Protestant followers of Jesus, being true to modernity's pursuit for ultimate knowledge, sparred over an endless minutia of doctrinal issues. Modernity's expectation was the realization of an ultimate truth, with the narcissistic implication being that one person's – or one church's – truth was correct. Therefore, everyone else was wrong. As a result, they effectively further divided themselves with each disagreement.

Over the next half a millennia, the result was tens of thousands of Protestant denominations and, along with them, greatly increased disunity and division. This trend towards division continues to this day. During the research stage of this work in 2008, there were a reported 38,000 Protestant denominations.[1] Towards

---

1. Yancey 2008, 119.

its conclusion in 2011, the number was pegged at 42,000.[2] This is an increase of over 10 percent in just three years, evidencing that division within Protestantism has not abated. The influence of modernity has been a particularly rough time for the church, in both practical and theological terms, serving to greatly exacerbate Christian disunity.

Moving from Modernism to Postmodernism

However, modernity is presently giving way to a postmodern perspective. While postmodernity is alternately vilified or ignored by much of the established church, it is nonetheless a real and relevant reality. Postmodern perspectives, while most prominently the property of the younger generations, are not a stage-of-life mindset from which one will grow out of and return to a modern point of view but, instead, a new lifelong outlook. Furthermore, although the transition from modernity to postmodernity is occurring at different rates around the world, it is indeed a global phenomenon. The key principles of the postmodern worldview are the dual tenants of two decidedly Christ-like characteristics: tolerance and acceptance. Today's Christian church is often viewed as being the opposite (intolerant and homogeneous), not accepting anyone who is or thinks differently. It is no wonder that society as a whole and especially postmodern constituents are quick to dismiss the modern-thinking church and its modern-thinking adherents.

With postmodernity comes an opportunity to correct modernity's errors and divisiveness, bringing with it a realistic hope for increased Christian unity. Though some will successfully resist it, most of Jesus' church is and will

---

2. Ted Olsen, "Go Figure," http://www.christianitytoday.com/ct/2011/april/gofigure-apr11.html, (accessed April 2, 2012) and "Status of Global Mission, 2011, in Context of 20th and 21st Centuries," http://www.gordonconwell.edu/resources/documents/StatusOfGlobalMission.pdf, (accessed April 2, 2012).

transition from modernity to postmodernity. In doing so, a new mindset with new paradigms and open-minded perspectives will emerge – among them greater tolerance and acceptance of those who act and think differently. Succinctly, postmodernism is the prescription for healing Christianity's homogeneous isolation and disunity.

Postmodern-thinking Christians, a population that continues to grow, do not fit in the modern Christian church. They are increasingly opting out of the traditional church structures of their parents and their youth – not leaving Jesus or rejecting their faith, but instead diligently and earnestly seeking a deeper, more meaningful manifestation of it. Often their quest becomes imperative, a compulsion to which they must yield to, less they spiritually die.

Early expressions of this pursuit have been found in what is called the emergent church or the emerging church. While some practitioners make distinctions between these two terms, doing so serves no purpose in aiding an understanding of the spiritual angst that underlies them. These movements – while possibly merely the next iteration of a seeker-sensitive service or, alternately, a short-lived expression preparing the way for something greater – are meaningful steps forward for postmodern Christians. A greater understanding of this is Phyllis Tickle's Great Emergence, which is notably occurring 500 years after the Reformation and may surpass its predecessor in both scope and influence.

Concisely, it is postmodernism, in general, and the Great Emergence, specifically, that provide a foundation on which Christian unity can be reclaimed and reestablished.

Another notable expression of postmodern-thinking Christians is the burgeoning house church movement. Within this effort there are different versions of house churches. These range from a traditional church that meets in a home and will one day grow to become an institutional church (a modern implementation) to the purposeful reclamation of the early church, with two millennia of manmade rules and expectations jettisoned (a postmodern implementation). For the latter, the Holy Spirit leads the service, with participants willingly and enthusiastically following. There are no sermons and any singing is spontaneous. Everyone is expected to participate, and everyone mutually ministers, serves, and receives.

In both the postmodern emergent movement and the postmodern implementation of the house church, a key outcome is an opportunity to leave behind the doctrinal disagreements and denominational divisions that modernity produced in abundance.

A 2,000-Year Prophetic Pattern

In concurrence with the Holy Spirit being the leader at many emergent gatherings and house church meetings, another interesting consideration is a bi-millennial pattern, a medieval prophecy as exemplified by Joachim of Fiore. After a 2,000-year era with a primary emphasis of God the Father, followed by a 2,000-year era focused on God the Son, we are embarking upon a new age of primary focus on God the Holy Spirit.

Thus we see an intersection of three events: a 500-year historic cycle, a 2,000-year prophetic pattern, and a new worldview, postmodernism. Three significant transitions are simultaneously occurring. These are a convergence of events.

Diverse Trinitarian Practices

An unfortunate consequence of Protestantism's 500-year history is that Christianity essentially and effectively has become a tritheistic faith in actual practice. While most Christians will vehemently deny this assertion, their words and their actions do much to belie their claim of innocence.

Protestantism, despite its 42,000 denominations, consists of three general streams of faith practices. These major factions are the liberals or mainlines, the evangelicals or fundamentalists, and the pentecostals and charismatics. Each one of these has a propensity to align and primarily identify with one member of the Christian Godhead – be it the Father, Son, or Spirit – while simultaneously diminishing the other two.

The first group, the mainlines, generally tends to place its focus on God the

Father. While the existence of Jesus and the Holy Spirit are understood as being part of the Trinity, it is more of a theoretical abstraction than a persistent reality. The mainline reverence for the Father is both right and admirable, yet in over identifying with Him there is a risk of syncretism (the acceptance and fusion of different belief systems), which can create unwarranted religious amalgamations. This heterogeneous practice, while often embracing other world religions, is not so accepting of Christianity's other two streams. The recommended prescription for the mainline and liberal churches is to likewise embrace Jesus and the Holy Spirit, just as they do God the Father.

In parallel fashion, the second group, the evangelicals, is predisposed to strongly identify with God the Son – that is, Jesus the Christ, the Messiah. Evangelicals focus on His saving nature and having a personal relationship with Him. This, too, is a correct and commendable course of Christian practice, yet when taken to excess, the result is dogmatic proclamations that, consistent with modernity's pursuit of ultimate knowledge, serve to divide and isolate them from others of differing perspectives. In their almost exclusive focus on Jesus, they can easily lose sight of the other two-thirds of the Trinity: God the Father and God the Holy Spirit. The recommended prescription for the evangelical and fundamental churches is to renew their pursuit and worship of the Father and the Holy Spirit, just as they do with Jesus.

The third and newest group, the charismatics, is inclined to concentrate on God the Holy Spirit. Charismatics pursue things such as the baptism of the Holy Spirit and speaking in tongues. Theirs is an experiential faith, which is subsequently reinforced through biblical study. In their thorough embrace of the Holy Spirit, the role of the Father and work of Jesus are diminished or overlooked. While the attention given to the power and movement of the Holy Spirit is a right and honorable reclamation of that which modernity removed from much of Christian practice, there is a real and present hazard of spiritualism creeping into their beliefs and practices. Although charismatics have admirably influenced many mainline and evangelical churches to reclaim Holy Spirit perspectives and practices, they too need more balance in their faith pursuits. The recommended prescription for charismatics and pentecostal churches is to recommit to the worship of God the Father and Jesus the Christ, just as they venerate the Holy Spirit.

While each of these three streams of Christianity has a correct and proper understanding relating to the part of the Godhead they emphasize, they are also at fault for not equally embracing the other two. Each faith faction needs to restore their beliefs and worship experiences to realize a balanced and God-honoring pursuit that truly embraces God as Trinity in actual practice.

In doing so, they do not need to abandon the history of their particular beliefs nor agree to banal uniformity, but they do each need to holistically seek the one true and living God who is revealed in Scripture as a three-person deity. As they seek to do so, their respective streams will coalesce, becoming a single river of a more unified Christianity.

Just as there is a convergence of events – with the 500-year historic cycle, 2,000-year prophetic pattern, and a new postmodern worldview – so, too, can there be an intentional convergence of worshiping God in a balanced Trinitarian manner as equal parts: Father, Jesus, and Holy Spirit. While the convergence of events is an inevitable development that is already set in motion and cannot be stopped, the convergence of worship is not a given. It must be diligently pursued by concerned Christians for it to be realized.

Taken in totality, the convergence of events and the convergence of worship can serve as the impetus for unity – that is, a convergence of Christian faith or a Great Convergence. These three convergences are shown in Table 3.

Table 3. Three Convergences

Convergence Type	Description	Notes
Convergence of Events (all occurring circa 2000 CE and manifesting in new forms of church practices):	A 500-year historic cycle	Moving into the Great Emergence
	A 2,000-year prophetic pattern	Moving into a primary focus on the Holy Spirit
	A new worldview	Moving from modernism to postmodernism
Convergence of Worship:	God the Father God the Savior God the Holy Spirit	God must be intentionally pursued in a balanced truly Trinitarian manner by all His followers.
The Great Convergence:	Realizing Christian Unity	The result of which will be the best, most effective witness to non-believers.

The Outcome

Postmodernism brings with it the potential to blur Christianity's historical lines of division, while the Great Emergence, with its leanings toward reclaiming the Holy Spirit, provides the proclivity to merge the three Christian theological silos of faith practices into an integrated whole. Even so, intentionality is required for a fuller realization of unity in Jesus. This comes in the form of comprehending and relentlessly pursuing a balanced Trinitarian understanding of the Godhead, allowing each of the major Protestant factions and their plethora of associated denominations to find commonality in the center of the Trinity, equally embracing God the Father, God the Son, and God the Holy Spirit.

With these evolving, reforming moves of postmodernism, the Great Emergence, and the pursuit of a balanced Trinitarianism come a potential reclamation of the oneness – that is, the unity – for which Jesus prayed, so that the "world may believe" (John 17:21).

As these two convergences – one inevitable: the convergence of events, and the other intentional: a convergence of worship – occur in tandem, the result will be a convergent Christian church, coming together as a unified one, just as Jesus and the Father are one (John 17:21) and for which He earnestly prayed (John 17:20-26).

This is the Great Convergence.

Why?

Quite simply and most importantly, so that the world may know Him (John 17:23). The Great Convergence will result in an optimal witness to others.

APPLICATIONS OF FINDINGS

The forward march of postmodernism is inevitable; it is not a temporary blip on history's timeline or a momentary occurrence that will later revert to modernism. Postmodernism is a significant global shifting of a worldview perspective. It is happening and will continue to occur without abatement, regardless of the degree or intensity of human assistance or opposition. Like the society in which they live, some Christians are postmodern.

As these burgeoning postmodern Christians apply their worldview to traditional church practices and the religious constructs of modernity, they yearn for more, for a fuller and more meaningful means to express the faith yearnings of their heart. This is being manifested in many ways, including the emergent church movement, house churches, and various parachurch organizations. Collectively these expressions of postmodern Christianity are called the Great Emergence.

With postmodernism as a veritable certainty, the continued unfolding of the Great Emergence is almost as likely. Major portions of Christianity will migrate towards the unifying centrality offered by the postmodern mindset of the Great Emergence, albeit with pockets of resistance residing uneasily on the periphery. These traditionalists will adamantly cling to a worldview and associated religious traditions mired in the remnants of modernity. While there will be a continued place for these modern Christians, they will be a decided minority, with postmodern Christians soon becoming the majority. However, just as pre-modern faith practices have persisted in the Modern Era, so, too, will modern practices exist in the Postmodern Era.

While no modern-thinking Christian should be forced into postmodern faith practices or structures, the converse is likewise inappropriate. It would be equally wrong to insist that postmodern Christians reside in a modern church where they do not belong. The modern church should let postmoderns go – with their blessings – even though the result will be a lessening of numbers and influence. Succinctly, postmoderns should not be forced into a modern box.

The reclamation of the Holy Spirit as a vital and integral part of postmodern faith and practice is a recurring theme throughout most of the manifestations of the Great Emergence that postmodern Christians have birthed. However, the Holy Spirit's role in these developments is not as inevitable a development as postmodernism or as likely as the Great Emergence.

Intentionality, therefore, is needed to more fully embrace the Holy Spirit. However, it is critical to do so without diminishing God the Father and God the Son, instead retaining all three as equals in a truly Trinitarian Godhead. This is the vision of pursuing a balanced Trinitarianism both in understanding and in actual practice, no longer segregating the Godhead in a tritheistic manner as is in actual evidence today by each of Christianity's three streams (mainline, evangelical, and charismatic). As Christians fully understand and actually embrace God as three-in-one, the segregated silos of Christian perspectives will melt away, resulting in them meeting at the center.

Together, this trio of movements – postmodernism, The Great Emergence, and the intentional pursuit of a holistic and true Trinitarianism – will serve to usher in a convergence of Christianity, a Great Convergence. It will possess the potential to fully result in the unity for which Jesus prayed. The ultimate outcome and intent of this Great Convergence is not establishing new institutions, amassing political influence, or creating worldly power structures, but simply "so that the world may believe" (John 17:21).

FURTHER STUDY

Some individuals may feel a philosophical pull or an intellectual interest in expanding the scope of this study beyond Christianity to consider a "convergence" with other world religions or of all the world's religions. While this may be a worthy pursuit for those advocating religious pluralism (an extremely postmodern ideal), it is not recommended by this researcher.

An intriguing subset of this pluralistic impulse is to consider those religions that emanate from or connect with the Old Testament of the Bible, specifically those which name Father Abraham as part of their religious heritage. These include Judaism, Christianity, Islam, and Mormonism. Doesn't each group worship the same God, albeit in vastly different ways? Should there be a mutual respect or affinity between these groups? What should one camp's attitude be towards the others? While there are many who would be aghast at such an inquiry, fearing it would extend convergence too far, an opposing group would criticize it for being too exclusive and not going far enough. They would, instead, advocate the convergence of all the world's religions.

Of greater value would be to explore past ecumenical movements, contrasting them with the Great Convergence. By examining the successes and failures of the past, along with their inherent strengths and weaknesses, the convergence movement can be bolstered and accelerated, with the intent to grow and perpetuate it – albeit in an organic and postmodern manner.

Perhaps the greatest and most needed consideration, however, is addressing how a balanced Trinitarianism can best be advocated and advanced within the church of Jesus. The imperative nature of this is that a failure to fully engage in a truly Trinitarian understanding of Father, Son, and Holy Spirit will serve to lessen the hope and opportunity to fully experience the answer to Jesus' prayer for unity. In this respect, Christian convergence – that is, Christian unity – can be either aptly aided or effectively thwarted by Jesus' followers simply by the manner in which they choose to worship the Trinitarian Godhead.

It is this researcher's hope and prayer that this work and others built upon it will rightly serve to aid and accelerate this convergence; that is, the unity of all who follow Jesus, so that the whole world may know (John 17:23-26).

APPENDIX A: DISPATCHES FROM THE EMERGENT FRONTIER

In his book *The New Christians: Dispatches from the Emergent Frontier,* Tony Jones takes readers on a journey into the emergent movement, interweaving twenty "dispatches" about this burgeoning phenomenon.

Dispatch 1: Emergents find little importance in the discrete differences between the various flavors of Christianity. Instead, they practice a generous orthodoxy that appreciates the contributions of all Christian movements.[1]

Dispatch 2: Emergents reject the politics and theologies of left versus right. Seeing both sides as a remnant of modernity, they look forward to a more complex reality.[2]

Dispatch 3: The gospel is like lava; no matter how much crust has formed over it, it will always find a weak point and burst through.[3]

Dispatch 4: The emergent phenomenon began in the late 1990s when a group of Christian leaders embarked on a conversation about how postmodernism was affecting faith.[4]

Dispatch 5: The emergent movement is not exclusively North American; it is

---

1. Jones 2008, 8.

2. Ibid., 20.

3. Ibid., 36.

4. Ibid., 41.

growing around the globe.[5]

Dispatch 6: Emergents see God's activity in all aspects of culture and reject the sacred-secular divide.[6]

Dispatch 7: Emergents believe that an envelope of friendship and reconciliation must surround all debates about doctrine and dogma.[7]

Dispatch 8: Emergents find the biblical call to community more compelling than the democratic call to individual rights. The challenge lies in being faithful to both ideals.[8]

Dispatch 9: The emergent movement is robustly theological. The conviction is that theology and practice are inextricably related, and each one invariably informs the other.[9]

Dispatch 10: Emergents believe that theology is local, conversational, and temporary. To be faithful to the theological giants of the past, emergents endeavor to continue their theological dialogue.[10]

Dispatch 11: Emergents believe that awareness of our relative position – to God, to one another, and to history – breeds biblical humility, not relativistic apathy.[11]

---

5. Ibid., 52.

6. Jones 2008, 75. In like manner, Rob Bell notes, "In the Hebrew Scriptures, there is no word for 'spiritual.' And Jesus never used the phrase 'spiritual life.' Because for Jesus and his tradition, all of life is spiritual." Bell 2007, Everything, back cover.

7. Jones 2008, 78.

8. Ibid., 81.

9. Ibid., 105. This is a balance between orthodoxy and orthopraxy.

10. Ibid., 111.

11. Ibid., 115.

Dispatch 12: Emergents embrace the whole Bible, both the glory and the pathos.[12]

Dispatch 13: Emergents believe that truth, like God, cannot be definitively articulated by finite human beings.[13]

Dispatch 14: Emergents embrace paradoxes, especially those that are core components of the Christian story.[14]

Dispatch 15: Emergents hold to a hope-filled eschatology: it was good news when Jesus came the first time, and it will be good news when He returns.[15]

Dispatch 16: Emergents believe that church should function more like an open-source network and less like a hierarchy or a bureaucracy.[16]

Dispatch 17: Emergents start new churches to save their own faith, not necessarily as an outreach strategy.[17]

Dispatch 18: Emergents firmly hold that God's Spirit – not their own efforts – is responsible for good in the world. The human task is to cooperate with God in what God is already doing.[18]

Dispatch 19: Emergents downplay – or outright reject – the differences between clergy and laity.[19]

Dispatch 20: Emergents believe that church should be just as beautiful and

---

12. Ibid., 144.

13. Ibid., 153.

14. Ibid., 163.

15. Ibid., 177.

16. Ibid., 180.

17. Ibid., 197.

18. Ibid., 202.

19. Jones 2008, 204. In like manner, Peter affirms the priesthood of all believers in 1 Peter 2:4-5.

messy as life.[20]

---

20. Jones 2008, 213.

Appendix B: The Revolution

The Trends Ushering in the "Revolution"

In his book *Revolution,* George Barna shares how a "quiet revolution" is taking place; he calls it the "Revolutionary Age." It is a "revolution of faith," a new, vibrant spirituality that is transcending the organized church.[1] He advances seven trends that are paving and have paved the path for this revolution.[2] They are:

1) **The Changing of the Guard**: The Baby Boom and Builder generations (the generation born prior to 1945, preceding the Babe Boomers) are yielding to the Buster (Gen-X) and Mosaic (Gen-Y or Millennial) generations.[3]

2) **The Rise of a New View of Life**: America is now a postmodern society, with no moral absolutes, a penchant for tolerance, and a proclivity for relationships.[4]

3) **Dismissing the Irrelevant**: There is a growing craving for relevance, jettisoning anything and everything that does not align with personal passions, while rejecting society's traditions, conventions, and social mores.[5]

---

1. Barna 2005, 9-11.

2. Ibid., 41-42.

3. Ibid., 42.

4. Ibid., 42-43.

5. Ibid., 43-44.

4) **The Impact of Technology**: Recent advances in technology have redefined how society lives and functions, changing the church in the process.[6]

5) **Genuine Relationships**: Younger generations highly value authentic and meaningful relationships and are willing to invest themselves in the lives of others. They are "people people," valuing teamwork and inclusiveness.[7]

6) **Participation in Reality**: Individuals have a growing desire to exert greater control over their lives and to be more cognizant of how they influence their world. They increasingly choose to match activities with personally rewarding results; they embrace faith dialogue and shared experience.[8]

7) **Finding True Meaning**: Sacrifice and surrender are emerging as the means to fulfillment and maturity, resulting in a meaningful existence.[9]

Passions of the Revolutionaries

Additionally, Barna cites seven passions of these revolutionaries, which are consistent with life in the early church. They are:

1) **Intimate Worship**: Daily worship God, in private and with others; this does not necessitate a worship service but is an attitudinal lifestyle of continual worship.

2) **Faith-Based Conversations**: People talk about what excites them; nothing should be more exciting than God.

3) **Intentional Spiritual Growth**: Faith is central to life and foundational to living.

4) **Servanthood**: The full manifestation of love is serving others by following Jesus' example.

5) **Resource Investment**: The attitude that our possessions are owned by God

---

6. Ibid., 44-45.

7. Ibid., 45-46.

8. Ibid., 46-47.

9. Ibid., 47.

and we merely serve as their manager. These resources are invested in the lives of other believers for their benefit.

6) **Spiritual Friendships**: The church is all about relationships, providing encouragement and promoting integrity through them.

7) **Family Faith**: God is central to the home and all that is done there; 2,000 years ago, the home essentially was the church.[10]

10. Ibid., 22-24.

APPENDIX C: MAJOR WORLDVIEW SHIFTS

Dan Kimball provides an overview of the different aspects of major historical worldviews; key portions of his chart are summarized in Table 4.[1]

Table 4: Historical Worldviews

Worldview	Ancient	Medieval	Modern	Postmodern
Era	2500 BCE to 500 CE	500 to 1500	1500 to 2000	2000
Foundational Understanding	Regional worldview; territorial deities	Judeo-Christian worldview; God-centered	Enlightenment; human-centric focus on reason	Pluralist view; tolerant of conflicting truth
Source of Power and Faith	Kings and local deities	The church	Human reason, science, logic	Personal experience
Communication Methodology	Oral	Oral / written	Printed word	Internet
Source of Authority	Revelation via oracles, kings, and prophets	Bible, as taught by the church; the Bible is kept from the people	Reason, logic, science; the Bible can be personally interpreted	Authority is questioned; the Bible is but one spiritual source
Prevailing Perspective	Man is insignificant	Believe to understand	Knowledge is power	Happiness is good

---

1. Kimball 2003, 44.

APPENDIX D: THE SEVEN PERSPECTIVES OF JESUS

Brian McLaren advances seven understandings of Jesus, which emanate from major streams of Christianity.[1] They are summarized in Table 5.

---

1. McLaren 2004, 49-74, specifically 72-73.

Table 5: Seven Perspectives of Jesus

Christian Perspective	Humanity's Problem	Jesus' Good News
Eastern Orthodox	Humanity is spiritually sick and needs healing	Jesus' incarnation brings healing to humanity and all creation
Roman Catholic	Humanity is enslaved by fear of death	Jesus' resurrection defeats death and liberates humanity
Anabaptist	Humanity is divided and violent, needing community in Jesus	Jesus exemplifies a learning community of disciples pursuing love and peace
Liberal Protestant	Humanity suffers from ignorance of Jesus' teachings and ways	Jesus' teaching and example provides inspiration to pursue social justice
Conservative Protestant	Humanity is guilty of sin	Jesus' death fully pays the penalty for sin
Pentecostal	Humanity is oppressed by disease and poverty	Jesus teaches how to receive healing and miracles from God, through faith
Nonviolent Liberation Theology	Humanity is oppressed by corrupted power and systems	Jesus' followers become activists to confront injustice and usher in peace

APPENDIX E: SOURCES OF ONGOING STUDY

Besides the resources listed in the Bibliography, the following are additional sources for further study and contemplation regarding the topics addressed in this dissertation.

Unity

Evangelism Reunion: Denominations and the Body of Christ, by John M. Frame. Grand Rapids: Baker, 1991.

The Social Sources of Denominationalism, by H. Richard Niebuhr. New York: Meridian, 1957.

www.scribd.com/doc/21009754/The-Greatest-Prayer-in-History: *The Greatest Prayer in History: John 17 Verse by Verse Commentary,* by Glenn Pease.

Church History

The Great Transformation: The Beginning of Our Religious Traditions, by Karen Armstrong. New York: Anchor Books, 2006.

Miller's Church History, by Andrew Miller. Addison: Bible Truth Publishers, 1980.

Re-forming the Center: American Protestantism, 1900 to the Present, by Douglas Jacobsen and William Trollinger. Grand Rapids: Wm. B Eerdmans Publishing, 1998.

Postmodern

After Virtue: A Study in Moral Theory, Third Edition, by Alistair MacIntyre. Notre Dame: University of Notre Dame Press, 2007.

All Things Are Spiritual, a video featuring Rob Bell, from "The Everything Is Spiritual" Tour. Grand Rapids, MI: Zondervan, 2007.

Beyond Fundamentalism and Liberalism: How Modern and Postmodern Philosophy Set the Theological Agenda, by Nancey Murphy. Philadelphia: Trinity Press International, 1996.

Beyond Fundamentalism: Shaping Theology in a Postmodern Context, by Stanley J. Grenz and John R. Franke. Louisville KY: Westminster/John Knox, 2001.

Four Views of Church in Postmodern Culture, by Leonard Sweet. Grand Rapids, MI: Zondervan, 2003.

The Last Word and the Word After That, by Brian D. McLaren. San Francisco: Jossey-Bass, 2005. (The third installment of a trilogy, which started with *A New Kind of Christian* and was followed by *The Story We Find Ourselves In.)*

A New Kind of Christian: A Tale of Two Friends on a Spiritual Journey, by Brian D. McLaren. San Francisco: Jossey-Bass, 2001.

A New Religious America: How a "Christian Country" Has Become the World's

Most Religiously Diverse Nation, by Diana Eck. New York: HarperCollins, 2002.

Postmodern Children's Ministry: Ministry to Children in the 21st Century, by Ivy Beckwith. Grand Rapids, MI: Zondervan, 2004.

The Postmodern Condition: A Report on Knowledge, Theory, and History of Literature, by Jean François Lytard. Minneapolis: University of Minnesota Press, 1948.

Postmodern Youth Ministry, by Tony Jones. El Cajon, CA: Youth Specialties, 2001.

A Primer on Postmodernism, by Stanley J. Genz. Grand Rapids, MI: Eerdmans, 1996.

Religious Education Between Modernism and Globalization, by Richard Robert Osmer and Freidrich Schweitzer. Grand Rapids, MI: Eerdmans, 2003.

Reverse Mentoring: How Young Leaders Can Transform the Church and Why We Should Let Them, by Earl Creps. San Francisco: Jossey-Bass, 2008.

Truth and the New Kind of Christian: The Emerging Effects of Postmodernism in the Church, by R. Scott Smith. Wheaton, IL: Crossway Books, 2005.

http://www.brianmclaren.net: "Brian D. McLaren is an author, speaker, pastor, and networker among innovative Christian leaders, thinkers, and activists."[1] He often addresses postmodernity, (as well as emergence).

Emergent

Alternative Worship: Resources from and for the Emerging Church, by Jonny

Baker and Doug Gay. Grand Rapids, MI: Baker, 2004.

Becoming Conversant with the Emerging Church: Understanding a Movement and Its Implications, by D. A. Carson. Grand Rapids, MI: Zondervan, 2005.

The Celtic Way of Evangelism, by George Hunter. Nashville, TN: Abingdon Press, 2000.

Changing Church: How God Is Leading His Church into the Future, by C. Peter Wagner. Ventura, CA: Regal 2004.

A Church for the 21st Century, by Leith Anderson. Minneapolis: Bethany, 1992.

Church in Emerging Culture: Five Perspectives, by Leonard Sweet, Andy Crouch, Brian D. McLaren, and Erwin Raphael McManus. Grand Rapids, MI: Zondervan, 2003.

Church Next: Quantum Changes in Christian Ministry, by Eddie Gibbs and Ian Coffey. Nottingham, UK: InterVarsity Press, 2001.

Deep Church: A Third Way Beyond Emerging and Traditional, by Jim Belcher. Downers Grove, IL: InterVarsity Press, 2009.

The Emergence of the Church: Context, Growth, Leadership and Worship, by Arthur G. Patzia. Downers Grove, IL: Intervarsity, 2001.

An Emergent Manifesto of Hope, by Doug Pagitt and Tony Jones. Grand Rapids, MI: Baker, 2007.

---

1. Accessed December 1, 2009.

The Emerging Christian Way: Thoughts, Stories, and Wisdom for a Faith of Transformation, Michael Schwartzentruber, editor. Kelowna, BC Canada: CopperHouse, 2006.

Exclusion and Embrace: A Theological Exploration of Identity, Openness, and Reconciliation, by Mirroslav Volf. Nashville, TN: Abingdon Press, 1996.

Future Church, by Jim Wilson. Littleton, CO: Serendipity, 2002.

God's Politics: Why the Right Gets It Wrong and the Left Doesn't Get It, by Jim Wallis. New York: HarperCollins Publishers, 2005.

The Heart of Christianity: Rediscovering a Life of Faith, by Marcus J. Borg. New York, NY: HarperOne, 2004.

Intuitive Leadership: Embracing a Paradigm of Narrative, Metaphor, and Chaos, by Tim Keel. Grand Rapids, MI: Baker Books, 2007.

The Irresistible Revolution: Living as an Ordinary Radical, Shane Claiborne. Grand Rapids: Zondervan, 2006.

Liquid Church, Pete Ward. Peabody, MA: Hendrickson Publishers, Inc: 2002.

Listening to the Beliefs of Emerging Churches: Five Perspectives, by Mark Driscoll, John Burke, Dan Kimball, Doug Pagitt, Karen Ward, and Robert Webber ed. Grand Rapids, MI: Zondervan, 2007.

The Lost Message of Jesus, by Steve Chalke and Alan Mann. Grand Rapids, MI: Zondervan, 2004.

Mission Shaped Church: Church Planting and Fresh Expressions of Church in a Changing Context, by Rowan Williams, et al. London: Church House, 2004.

The Missional Church: A Vision for the Sending of the Church in North America, Darrell Guder, ed. Grand Rapids, MI: Eerdmans, 1998.

The Post-Evangelical, by Dave Tomlinson. Grand Rapids, MI: Zondervan, 2003.

The Quest of the Historical Jesus, by Albert Schweitzer. London: Adam & Charles Black, 1954.

Reimaging Spiritual Formation: A Week in the Life of an Experimental Church, by Doug Pagitt. Grand Rapids, MI: Zondervan, 2004.

Reinventing American Protestantism: Christianity in the New Millennium, by Donald E. Miller. Los Angeles: University of California Press, 1999.

The Second Reformation, by William A. Beckham. Houston: Touch Publications, 1995.

Stories of Emergence, Michael Yaconelli, ed. El Cajon, CA: Emergent YS, 2003.

An Unstoppable Force: Daring to Become the Church God Had in Mind, by Erwin Raphael McManus. Loveland, CO: Group, 2001.

Why We're Not Emergent: By Two Guys Who Should Be, by and Ted Kluck. Chicago: Moody Publishers, 2008.

Worship in the Early Church, by Ralph P. Martin. Grand Rapids, MI: Eerdmans, 1964.

http://djchuang.googlepages.com/WeKnowMoreThanOurPastors.pdf: "We Know More Than Our Pastors," an online whitepaper by Tim Bednar.

http://anglimergent.ning.com and
http://www.facebook.com/group.php?gid=2380264196: "A relational network
of Anglicans engaging emerging church & mission."[2]

http://baptimergent.wordpress.com: "An Emergent Baptist Network."[3]

http://blog.beliefnet.com/jesuscreed: "Scot McKnight is a widely-recognized
authority on the New Testament, early Christianity, and the historical Jesus. He
is the Karl A. Olsson Professor in Religious Studies at North Park University
(Chicago, Illinois). A popular and witty speaker, Dr. McKnight has given
interviews on radios across the nation, has appeared on television, and is regularly
asked to speak in local churches and educational events. Dr. McKnight obtained
his Ph.D. at the University of Nottingham (1986)."[4]

http://luthermergent.ning.com: "Luthermergent is a network of friends
committed to both the emergent and Lutheran tribes."[5]

http://mereorthodoxy.com: "a place where readers of all ages can gather to think
deeply about the truth of the Christian faith with respect to the culture around
us."[6]

http://methomergentlab.wordpress.com: "a place for generative conversation
among those who want to make a difference in the United Methodist Church."[7]

http://phyllistickle.com: Phyllis Tickle "is an authority on religion in America
and a much sought after lecturer on the subject."[8]

http://presbymergent.org and http://www.facebook.com/Presbymergent:

---

2. Accessed November 23, 2009.

3. Accessed November 27, 2009.

"Presbymergent is the online community for those who live in both the Presbyterian (PCUSA) and Emergent/emerging church worlds and want to try and find a balance between the two."

http://synagogue3000.org and http://synagogue3000.org/synablog: Seeks to be a mechanism to help Jewish congregations and communities "create synagogues that are sacred and vital centers of Jewish life."[9] In simplistic terms, this is Jewish emergence.

http://tallskinnykiwi.typepad.com/tallskinnykiwi: Andrew Jones: "I am quite tall (6.5) quite skinny and was born in New Zealand (Kiwi). I have been a mission consultant for the last decade and a social entrepreneur for...two decades."[10]

http://young.anabaptistradicals.org: "a loose affiliation of self-identified young Anabaptist radicals."[11]

www.alternativeworship.org: A portal site for alternative forms of worship (and the emergent church).

www.dianabutlerbass.com: website of religion author Diana Butler Bass.

www.emergingchurch.info: A portal site for the emergent church movement.

---

4. Accessed November 23, 2009.

5. Accessed November 27, 2009.

6. Accessed December 14, 2009.

7. Accessed November 27, 2009.

8. Accessed November 27, 2009.

www.emerginglutherans.org: A place where "Lutherans and others can engage the emerging conversation."[12]

www.emergentvillage.com / www.emergentvillage.org: "Emergent Village is a growing, generative friendship among missional Christians seeking to love our world in the Spirit of Jesus Christ";[13] its founding purpose is as an "egalitarian social-networking organization."[14]

www.freshworship.org: a Christian alternative worship community/network.

www.next-wave.org: a resource covering "next wave of church and culture."[15]

www.smallritual.org: Steve Collins addresses the emerging church and related topics.

www.theooze.com: articles about the emerging church.

www.vintagefaith.com and www.dankimball.com: a blog and resource by Dan Kimball, author of *The Emerging Church.*

www.youthspecialties.com: a resource for emerging ministry with youth (and adults).

Also, consider the writings and teachings of theologians Jürgen Moltmann and Miroslav Volf, who have influenced many emergents.[16]

---

9. Accessed December 21, 2009.

10. Accessed November 23, 2009.

11. Accessed November 27, 2009.

12. Accessed November 23, 2009.

Small Groups

Building a Church of Small Groups, by Bill Donahue and Russ Robinson. Grand Rapids, MI: Zondervan, 2001.

Cell Groups and House Churches, by Peter Bunton. Ephrata, PA: House to House Publications: 2001.

Growing People Through Small Groups, by David Stark and Betty Veldman Wieland. Grand Rapids, MI: Bethany House Publishers, 2004.

Nine Keys to Effective Small Group Leadership, by Carl F. George. Mansfield, PA: Kingdom Publishing, 1997.

Prepare Your Church for the Future, by Carl F. George. Grand Rapids, MI: Fleming H. Revell, 1992.

Walking the Small Group Tightrope, by Bill Donahue and Russ Robinson. Grand Rapids, MI: Zondervan, 2003.

House Churches

Cell Groups and House Churches, by Peter Bunton. Ephrata, PA: House to House Publications: 2001.

Church 3.0: Upgrades for the Future of the Church, by Neil Cole. San Francisco: Jossey-Bass, 2010.

The Church in the House: A Return to Simplicity, by Robert Fitts. Salem, OR: Preparing the Way Publishers, 2001.

The Church in Your House, by Victor Choudhrie. 2006. (This book lists no publisher and is distributed by the author. As of December 2009, it is available at http://www.1040win.com/resources/books.htm.)

House Church Networks: A Church for a New Generation, by Larry Kreider. Lititz, PA: House to House Publications, 2007.

Houses That Change the World, by Wolfgang Simson. Authentic Media, 2005.

Natural Church Development: A Guide to Eight Essential Qualities of Healthy Churches, by Christian A. Schwarz. Churchsmart Resources, 1996.

The Open Church: How to Bring Back the Exciting Life of the First Century Church, by James Rutz. 1992 (this book is apparently out of print, but used copies are available online).

Reimaging Spiritual Formation: A Week in the Life of an Experimental Church, by Doug Pagitt. Grand Rapids, MI: Zondervan, 2004.

Rethinking the Wineskin: The Practice of the New Testament Church, by Frank Viola. Brandon, FL: Present Testimony Ministry, 2001.

Simply Church, by Tony and Felicity Dale. Austin, TX: Karis Publishing, 2002.

The Way the Church Ought to Be/Volume I: Ninety-five Propositions for a Return to Radical Christianity, by Robert A. Lund. Albany, OR: Outside the Box Press, 2001.

Who Is Your Covering, by Frank Viola. Brandon, FL: Present Testimony Ministry, 1998.

www.house2house.com: "a website designed to help any within the simple/organic church."[17]

www.housechurch.org: a resource for house churches.

www.house-church.org: "explain the concept of Biblical Church, and to encourage a return to the teaching of the Word of God."[18]

www.intentionaleucharisticcommunities.org: "Intentional Eucharistic Communities (IECs) are those small faith communities, rooted in the Catholic tradition, which gather to celebrate Eucharist on a regular basis."[19]

www.megashiftministries.org: "To launch and nurture open fellowships," creating "mature Christian disciples" in the process.[20]

http://www.simplechurch.com: "a Social Networking site for those involved in or interested in simple expressions of church."[21]

Other

The Hip-Hop Church: Connections with the Movement Shaping Our Culture, by Efra Smith and Phil Jackson. InterVarsity Press, 2005.

Joachim of Fiore and the Prophetic Future, by Marjorie Reeves. Sutton Publishing, 1999.

The Starfish and the Spider: The Unstoppable Power of Leaderless Organizations, by Ori Brafman and Rod A. Beckstrom. Portfolio Trade: 2008.

---

17. Accessed December 19, 2009.

18. Accessed December 19, 2009.

BIBLIOGRAPHY

The American Heritage Dictionary. Boston: Houghton Mifflin Company, 1985.

Anderson, Troy. "Charismatic Renewal Marks 50 Years." *Charisma* (April 2010).

Armstrong, Chris R. *Patron Saints for Postmoderns.* Downers Grove, IL: InterVarsity Press, 2009.

Bailey, Sarah Pulliam. "A Voice for Sanity." *Christianity Today* (November 2009).

Barclay, William. *The Gospel of John.* Vol. 2. Philadelphia: Westminster Press, 1975.

Barna, George. *The Barna Report: What Americans Believe.* Ventura, CA: Regal, 1991.

Barna, George. *Revolution.* Carol Stream, IL: Tyndale House Publishers, 2005.

Barna, George, and Frank Viola. "Life Today with Ted Griffin." Audio podcast interview by Ted Griffin (recorded April 8, 2008), http://www.ptmin.org/barna_viola2.mp3 (accessed November 17, 2009).

Barton, Ruth Haley. "Make a Joyful Silence." *Sojourners* (February 2009).

Bass, Diana Butler. *Christianity for the Rest of Us: How the Neighborhood Church Is Transforming the Faith.* New York: HarperOne, 2006.

Bass, Diana Butler. "Emergence Meets Mainline." Emergent Village podcast (June 2, 2007), http://www.emergentvillage.com/podcast/mainline-churches-engage-the-emerging-conversation (accessed December 21, 2009).

Bass, Diana Butler. *A People's History of Christianity: The Other Side of the Story.* New York: HarperOne, 2009.

Bass, Diana Butler. *The Practicing Congregation: Imagining a New Old Church.* Herndon, VA: The Alban Institute, 2004.

Bean, Lydia. "Bridging the Great Divide." *Sojourners* (March 2009).

Beaty, Katelyn. "Lost in Translation." *Christianity Today* (October 2009).

Beliefnet. http://blog.beliefnet.com/jesuscreed/2006/11/bloglossary.html (accessed October 20, 2010).

Bell, Rob. *Everything Is Spiritual.* Zondervan, 2007. DVD.

Bell, Rob. *Sex God: Exploring the Endless Connections between Sexuality and Spirituality.* Grand Rapids, MI: Zondervan, 2007.

Bell, Rob. Audio sermon podcast at Mars Hill Bible Church (November 9, 2008).

Bennett, Dennis. "God's Strength for This Generation." *Sojourners* (April 2010).

Berger, Rose Marie. "Radical Possibility." *Sojourners* (February 2009).

Bushnell, Horace. *Building Eras in Religion.* Charleston, SC: Nabu Press, 2010.

Chenoweth, Gregg, and Caleb Benoit. "Where Jerusalem and Mecca Meet." *Christianity Today* (July 2009).

Clark, Jeff. "Postmodern World." *Charisma* (May 2009).

Conder, Tim, and Daniel Rhodes. *Free for All: Rediscovering the Bible in Community.* Grand Rapids, MI: Baker Books, 2009.

Conger, George. "Second Thoughts on Syncretism." *Christianity Today* (May 2009).Crowder, John. *Miracle Workers, Reformers, and the New Mystics.* Shippensburg, PA: Destiny Publishers Inc., 2006.

Dale, Tony, Felicity Dale, and George Barna. *The Rabbit and the Elephant: Why Small Is the New Big for Today's Church.* USA: Barna Books/Tyndale House Publishers, 2009.

D'Souza, Dinesh. "The Clash of Stereotypes." *Christianity Today* (July 2009).

Egeler, Daniel. *Mentoring Millennials: Shaping the Next Generation.* Colorado Springs, CO: Navpress, 2003.

Frame, John M. *Evangelism Reunion: Denominations and the Body of Christ.* Grand Rapids, MI: Baker, 1991.

Frangipane, Francis. "All We Need Is Jesus." *Charisma* (November 2009).

Franke, John R. "Reforming Theology: Toward a Postmodern Reformed Dogmatics," http://www.nextreformation.com/wp-admin/resources/Reforming_Theology.pdf (accessed December 7, 2009).

The Free Dictionary. http://www.thefreedictionary.com.

Friedman, Thomas L. *The World Is Flat: A Brief History of the Twenty-first Century.* New York: Farrar, Straus & Giroux, 2005.

Gains, Adrienne S. "ORU to Host Global Pentecostal Congress." *Charisma* (March 2010).

Galli, Mark. "In the Beginning, Grace." *Christianity Today* (October 2009).

Galli, Mark. "Reasoning Together." *Christianity Today* (August 2009).

Gibbs, Eddie, and Ryan Bolger. *Emerging Churches: Creating Christian Communities in Postmodern Cultures.* Grand Rapids, MI: Baker Academic, 2005.

Glazier, Chris. "Promise Keepers Expands Focus in 2009." *Charisma* (June 2009).

Grady, J. Lee. *The Holy Spirit Is Not For Sale: Rekindling the Power of God in an Age of Compromise.* Grand Rapids, MI: Chosen Books, 2010.

Grady, J. Lee. "Passing the Torch." *Charisma* (April 2010).

Green, Matthew. "The Church Dropout." *Charisma* (December 2009).

Guthrie, Stan. "All Monotheisms Are Not Alike." *Christianity Today* (November 2008).

Hsu, Al. "Family Ties." *Christianity Today* (December 2008).

Hutchinson, Mary. "Ministry Centralizes Haiti Outreaches." *Charisma*

(September 2009).

The Internet Movie Database. http://www.imdb.com/title/tt0133093/quotes (accessed November 23, 2009).

Johnson, Bill. "Wisdom's Tension." Audio sermon podcast, Bethel Church (February 16, 2009).

Jones, Tony. *The New Christians: Dispatches from the Emergent Frontier.* San Francisco: Jossey-Bass, 2008.

Kennedy, John W. "The Ultimate Kibitzer." *Christianity Today* (February 2009).

Khan, Daisy. "Balancing Tradition with Pluralism." *Sojourners* (February 2009).

Kimball, Dan. *The Emerging Church: Vintage Christianity for New Generations.* Grand Rapids, MI: Zondervan, 2003.

Kimball, Dan. *They Like Jesus But Not The Church: Insights from Emerging Generations.* Grand Rapids, MI: Zondervan, 2007.

Loveless, Josh. "Church Mutiny." *Relevant* (November/December 2009).

Ma, Jaeson. "The Reverse Flow of Missions." *Relevant* (January/February 2010). (It is unclear whether Jaeson Ma is the author or merely the source for this article.)

McArthur, John. *The McArthur Bible Commentary.* Nashville, TN: Thomas Nelson, 2005.

McHugh, Adam S. *Introverts in the Church: Finding Our Place in an Extroverted Culture.* Downers Grove, IL: InterVarsity Press, 2009.

McLaren, Brian D. *Finding Faith: A Self-Discovery Guide for Your Spiritual Quest*. Grand Rapids, MI: Zondervan, 1999.

McLaren, Brian D. *A New Kind of Christian: A Tale of Two Friends on a Spiritual Journey*. San Francisco, CA: Jossey-Bass, 2001.

McLaren, Brian D. *The Story We Find Ourselves In: Further Adventures of a New Kind of Christian*. San Francisco, CA: Jossey-Bass, 2003.

McLaren, Brian D. *A Generous Orthodoxy*. Grand Rapids, MI: Zondervan, 2004.

McLaren, Brian D. *Everything Must Change: Jesus, Global Crises, and a Revolution of Hope*. Nashville, TN: Thomas Nelson, 2007.

McNeal, Reggie. *The Present Future: Six Tough Questions for the Church*. San Francisco: Jossey-Bass, 2003.

Miller, Donald E. "Rethinking Church: Learning from new paradigm congregations," http://www.thunderstruck.org/holysmoke/rethinkingchurch.htm (accessed February 6, 2010).

Miller, Lisa. "House of Worship." *Newsweek* (January 11, 2010), http://www.newsweek.com/id/228722 (accessed January 14, 2010).

Miller, Lisa. "We Are All Hindus Now." *Newsweek* (August 31, 2009), http://www.newsweek.com/id/212155 (accessed January 7, 2010).

Millner, Rev. Marlon, and Dr. Paul Alexander. "Public Spirit." *Sojourners* (June 2009).

Morgan, Timothy C. "After the Aloha Shirts." *Christianity Today* (October

2008).

Mouw, Richard. "Dr. Richard Mouw." Audio sermon podcast, Hope College, The Gathering service (October 26, 2008).

Mouw, Richard. "Dr. Richard Mouw." Audio sermon podcast, Hope College, Chapel service (October 27, 2008).

Neff, David. "Ardor and Order." *Christianity Today* (May 2010).

Nouwen, Henri. *Bread for the Journey.* New York: HarperCollins, 1997.

O'Brien, Brandon. "Emergent's Divergence." *Christianity Today* (January 2009).

Olsen, Ted. "Go Figure," http://www.christianitytoday.com/ct/2011/april/gofigure-apr11.html (accessed April 2, 2012).

The Ooze: Evolving Spirituality. http://www.theooze.com/articles/article.cfm?id=1151 (accessed October 20, 2010).

Pagitt, Doug. *A Christianity Worth Believing: Hope-Filled, Open-Armed, Alive-and-Well Faith.* San Francisco: Jossey-Bass, 2008.

Pagitt, Doug. *Reimaging Spiritual Formation: A Week in the Life of an Experimental Church.* Grand Rapids, MI: Zondervan, 2003.

Porte, Jeff. http://www.thirdreformed.orginside.php?a=PG:207 (accessed August 27, 2008).

Rah, Soong-Chan. *The Next Evangelism.* Downers Grove, IL: InterVarsity Press,

2009.

Rutz, James. *Mega Shift: Igniting Spiritual Power*. Colorado Springs, CO: Empowerment Press, 2005.

Sande, Ken. *The Peacemaker*, 4th ed. Grand Rapids, MI: Baker Books, 2005.

Schwarz, Christian A. *The Threefold Art of Experiencing God: The Liberating Power of a Trinitarian Faith*. Carol Stream, IL: ChurchSmart Resources, 1999.

Simson, Wolfgang. *The House Church Book: Rediscover the Dynamic, Organic, Relational, Viral Community Jesus Started*. USA: Tyndale/Barna Books, 2009.

"Status of Global Mission, 2011, in Context of 20th and 21st Centuries," http://www.gordonconwell.edu/resources/documents/StatusOfGlobalMission .pdf, (accessed April 2, 2012).

Strang, Stephen. "Good News for Charismatics." *Charisma* (June 2009).

Tchividjian, Tullian. *Unfashionable: Making a Difference in the World by Being Different*. Colorado Springs, CO: Multnomah Books, 2009.

Tickle, Phyllis. "Ancient Disciplines for the Church." Audio sermon podcast, Mars Hill Bible Church (June 29, 2008). Tickle, Phyllis. "A Conversation with Phyllis Tickle." Audio podcast interview by Tony Jones and Doug Pagitt, Emergent Village (March 12, 2008), ttp://www.emergentvillage.com/podcast/.

Tickle, Phyllis. *The Great Emergence: How Christianity Is Changing and Why*. Grand Rapids, MI: Baker Books, 2008.

Tickle, Phyllis. "Phyllis Tickle interviewed by Tony Jones." Audio podcast, Emergent Village (July 15, 2007), http://www.emergentvillage.com/podcast/.

Tickle, Phyllis. "A Treasure We Don't Understand." Audio sermon podcast, Mars Hill Bible Church (May 3, 2009).

Tickle, Phyllis. *The Words of Jesus: A Gospel of the Sayings of Our Lord.* San Francisco: Jossey-Bass, 2008.

Vallotton, Kris, and Bill Johnson. *The Supernatural Ways of Royalty: Discovering Your Rights and Privileges of Being a Son or Daughter of God.* Shippensburg, PA: Destiny Publishers Inc., 2006.

Van Duzer, Nate. "Building Bridges." *Sojourners* (February 2009).

Vieira, Paul. *Jesus Has Left the Building.* Woodland Park, CO: Karis Publishing, 2006.

Viola, Frank. "The House Church Movement: Learning from the Past, Pioneering for the Future." Audio podcast, House2House Conference, Dallas (2007).

Viola, Frank. *Reimagining Church.* Colorado Springs, CO: David C. Cook, 2008.

Viola, Frank, and George Barna. *Pagan Christianity?: Exploring the Roots of Our Church Practices.* USA: Tyndale House Publishers Inc., 2008.

Wagner, C. Peter. *Changing Church: How God Is Leading His Church into the Future.* Ventura, CA: Regal Books, 2004.

Wagner, C. Peter. *Warfare Prayer: How to Seek God's Power and Protection in the Battle to Build His Kingdom.* Ventura, CA: Regal Books, 1992.

Wallis, Jim. *The Great Awakening.* New York: HarperCollins Publishers, 2008.

Walvoord, John F. and Roy B. Zuck. *The Bible Knowledge Commentary: An Exposition of the Scriptures by Dallas Seminary Faculty, New Testament Edition.* Colorado Springs, CO: David C. Cook, 1983.

Warren, Rick. *The Purpose Driven Life.* Grand Rapids, MI: Zondervan, 2002.

Wikipedia. http://en.wikipedia.org.

Yancey, Phillip. "Denominational Diagnostics." *Christianity Today* (November 2008).

Yancey, Phillip. *The Jesus I Never Knew.* Grand Rapids, MI: Zondervan, 1995.

Yancey, Phillip. "O, Evangelicos!" *Christianity Today* (December 2009).

Yung, Hwa. "A 21st Century Reformation: Recover the Supernatural." *Christianity Today* (September 2010).